Power and Influence

Power and Influence:
Enhancing Information Services
within the Organization

Guy St Clair

BOWKER
SAUR

London • Melbourne • Munich • New Jersey

British Library Cataloguing in Publication Data

St. Clair, Guy
  Power and Influence: Enhancing
  Information Services within the
  Organization. - (Information Services
  Management Series)
  I. Title II. Series
  025.1

  ISBN 1-85739-098-9

Library of Congress Cataloging-in-Publication Data

St. Clair, Guy, 1940-
  Power and influence : enhancing information services within the
organization / Guy St. Clair.
       p.   cm. -- (Information services management series)
  Includes bibliographical references (p.   ) and index.
  ISBN 1-85739-098-9 (acid-free paper)
  1. Information services--United States--Management. I. Title.
II. Series.
Z674.5.U5S7 1994
025.1'0973--dc20
                                                          94-32284
                                                              CIP

Published by Bowker-Saur Limited
Maypole House, Maypole Road
East Grinstead, West Sussex RH19 1HH, UK
Tel: +44 (0) 342 330100. Fax: +44 (0) 342 330191

Bowker-Saur is a division of REED REFERENCE PUBLISHING

ISBN 1-85739-098-9

Cover design by Juan Hayward
Typesetting by Florencetype Ltd, Stoodleigh, Devon
Printed on acid-free paper
Printed and bound in Great Britain by Bookcraft (Bath) Ltd

The author

Guy St Clair is the president of SMR International, a management consulting, training and publishing company with offices in New York. The company's clients include major chemical, pharmaceutical and engineering firms, and information organizations connected with the federal government, medicine, the arts, and the academic community. SMR International also publishes *InfoManage: The International Management Newsletter for the Information Services Executive* and, through its subsidiary company, OPL Resources Ltd, *The One-Person Library: A Newsletter for Librarians and Management*. In London, the company is represented by TFPL Ltd, through which the services of SMR International are offered to the European market.

Formerly an adjunct lecturer at the Catholic University of America in Washington DC, Guy St Clair has taught graduate seminars on the information center/special library and on library and information management. He has also been a visiting lecturer at the University of Washington in Seattle. A past president of the Special Libraries Association (1991–1992), Guy St Clair is an alumnus of the University of Virginia (BA), with graduate work at the University of Illinois (MSLS). He lives in New York City.

This book is dedicated to
Andrew Berner

. . . and to two fine colleagues and friends,
David R. Bender and Nigel Oxbrow,
both of whom understand
power and influence
in the information environment

Introduction to the series

A broader management perspective for information services

For several years, decades it seems, librarians and other information services professionals have lamented the fact that there is not enough emphasis on management in their training. They learn their subjects, and librarians, especially, connect very early on in their training to the concepts of service and the organization of information. Management skills, however, are frequently neglected, or given minimal attention, and many information services professionals find themselves working in the corporate environment, research and technology organizations, government information units, or community/public administration organizations where management skills are needed. Much of what they need they get on the job; other approaches, such as continuing education programs, are utilized by those who have the initiative to recognize that they must do something to educate themselves to be managers. Some of it works and some of it does not.

Bowker-Saur's *Information Services Management Series*, for which I serve as Series Editor, seeks to address this need in the information services community. For this series (and indeed, since the entire field of information management is strongly predicted by many to be going in this direction), the concept of information services is being defined very broadly. The time has come, it seems to me, to recognize that the various constituent units of our society concerned with information have many of the same goals, objectives, and not surprisingly, many of the same concerns. The practice of management is one of these, and for our purposes, it does not matter if the reader of these books is employed as an information manager, information provider, information specialist, or indeed, as an information counsellor (as these information workers have been described by one of the leaders of business and industry). In fact, it does not matter whether the reader is employed in information technology, telecommunications, traditional librarianship, records management, corporate or organizational archives, the information brokerage field, publishing, consulting, or any of the myriad branches of information services (including service to the information community and the many vendors who make up that branch of the profession). These new titles on the management of information services have been chosen specifically for their value to all who are part of this community of information workers.

While much work is being done in these various disciplines, little of it concentrates on management, and that which is done generally concentrates on one or another of the specific subgroups of the field. This series seeks to unite management concepts throughout information services, and while some of the titles will be directed to a specific group, most will be broad-based and will attempt to address issues of concern to all information services employees. For example, one of the projected titles has to do with entrepreneurial librarianship, which would seem to be limited to the library profession, but in fact the book will offer information and guidance of use to anyone working in the information services field who is willing to incorporate entrepreneurial thinking into his or her work.

It will be pointed out, of course, that the practice of management in information services is addressed within the organizations or communities which employ information workers. This is true, and certainly in the corporate world (and, arguably, in the public and academic library communities as well), there are plenty of occasions for information services employees to participate in management training as provided in-house. There is nothing wrong with that approach, and in many organizations it works very well, but the training does not proceed from an information services point of view, thus forcing the information worker to adapt, as best he or she can, the management practices of the organization to the management practices needed for the best provision of information services. The titles to appear in the Bowker-Saur *Information Services Management Series* will enable the information worker to relate *information* management to *organizational* management, thus putting the information worker (especially the information executive) in a position of considerable strength in the organization or community where he or she is employed. By understanding management principles (admittedly, as frequently 'borrowed' from the general practice of management) and relating them to the way the information services unit is organized, the information services employee not only positions himself or herself for the better provision of information services, but the entire information services unit is positioned as a respectable participant in organizational or community operations.

This last point perhaps needs some elaboration, for it should be made clear that the books in the series are not intended exclusively for the corporate or specialized information services field. It is our intention to provide useful management criteria for all kinds of information services, including those connected to public, academic, or other publicly supported libraries. Our basic thesis is that quality management leads to quality services, regardless of whether the information services activity is privately of publicly funded, whether it is connected with a private research institution or a public governmental agency, or indeed, whether it is a temporary information unit or whether it is part of a permanently funded and staffed operation. Writing for this series will be authors, who, I am sure, will challenge some of the usual barriers to effective management practices in this or that type of library or information services unit, and certainly there will be librarians, records managers, archivists and others who will be able to relate some of their management practices in such a way that CIOs and computer services managers will benefit from the telling. In other words, our attempt here is to clear away the usual preconceptions about management within the various branches of information services, to do away with the very concept of 'well-that-might-work-for-you-but-it-won't-work-for-me' kind of thinking. We can no longer afford to fight turf battles about whether or not management is 'appropriate' in one or another of the various subunits of information provision. What we must do, and what the *Information Services Management Series* expects to do, is to bring together the best of all of us, and to share our management expertise so that we all benefit.

Guy St Clair
Series Editor

Contents

Foreword

Politics is a driving force in every organizational setting, whether it be that of the nation's highest legislative body or that of the information services provider. Just as a member of Congress must learn how to shape a law from the introduction of a bill to its successful enactment, in this time of increased competition within organizations for resources, success depends on the ability of the information professional to work the political system within the organization. It is not unusual for a junior member to spend years learning the intricate steps in the dance of legislation. It is also not by chance that the chairmanship of a powerful congressional committee goes to a senior member who has established an intricate network of powerful contacts to help him achieve his goals.

While each organization is different, Guy St. Clair, the twentieth century Machiavelli for the information professional, creates a roadmap to success in this book, the second in the *Information Services Management Series*. The principles outlined here can be applied to any type of workplace, and the techniques recommended are similar to those used by elected officials who must build support for government policies and programs.

Mr St. Clair emphasizes the importance of building a base of support within the organization that involves networking, strategic partnerships, and personal relationships with those who are the organization's key decision makers. Information professionals are placed in a unique position to do this since they are the gatekeepers to the key component which decision makers need – information. Marvin J. Cetron, a noted futurist, has predicted that a typical business by the year 2000 will have more than 40 percent of the workforce involved in collecting, analyzing, synthesizing, structuring, storing, or retrieving information.

Developing strategies and designing and delivering services which meet the needs of the constituency depend on paying attention to what constituent users are saying, listening to their discussions of both short and long term objectives, anticipating their information needs, and adjusting as new directions arise. This vision of service takes *what* service means seriously. But while that accounts for the quality factor, quality service does not sell itself.

In that part of his book entitled 'Seeking influence and finding advocates' (Chapters 8–10), Mr St. Clair emphasizes clearly the importance of getting out the message that *we're here to help you*. Only when the information center has strong advocates within itself and in other areas of the organization will it be able to thrive and grow. Just as in Congress, where resource allocation decisions are made on the basis of which coalition or interest group presents the most compelling cause, so too in the workplace, the voices which are strongest will prevail. It is not enough to have the silent majority as constituent users. They need to be mobilized into a proactive force which is convinced that helping the information provider is helping themselves.

Catherine A. Jones
Chief, Congressional Reference Division
Congressional Research Service
The Library of Congress, Washington DC and
Adjunct Professor, School of Library and Information Science
The Catholic University of America, Washington DC

Introduction
Power and influence in information services

We are no longer looking *toward* the much-anticipated and much-discussed 'information age', we are there. The information age has arrived, whether we like it or not and whether we are comfortable with it or not. The forces in society that influence how money is spent on information services and products now react to information issues just as they have always reacted to any other issues affecting the delivery of any other products and services. In today's society, accountability is all.

In the modern, well managed organization, justification is required for every expenditure, regardless of how meritorious or beneficial that expenditure might be, and in information services management, justifying the products and services provided for users is equally required. The justification of information services (or, as I prefer to think of it, the *validation* of those services) is based solely on the value of the services to the organization or community which supports the information services unit. The information services manager who succeeds is the one who knows the value of information services to the organization or community, who knows how to convey that value to the decision makers, and who understands the techniques for enhancing the value of the information. Today, there is no *more* money, but there is plenty of money already available for those products and services which can be demonstrated – to those who control the financial process – to be of value.

This book is about the management of information services and how the successful management of information services is achieved. The basic thesis of the book is that, when accepted and applied to information services, certain societal characteristics play a major role in determining whether or not the information services organization will be acknowledged, supported, and indeed empowered to provide the information products and services it was created to provide. The application of such concepts as advocacy, political sponsorship, mentoring and the establishment of strategic and mutually beneficial partnerships can have a mighty impact on the successful provision of information. The appropriate incorporation of these concepts and strategies into the day-to-day workings of the information services unit can, and will, lead to power and influence. With power and influence comes empowerment, and with empowerment, the success of the unit and its employees in doing what they have been appointed to do, to provide the highest levels of information services that they can provide.

Although I have for many years believed that the true source of power and influence in information services lies with the relationships information workers have with their users, managers and peers, the concepts which led to this book are not all original to me. Many people write about mentoring and strategic partnerships, and certainly in other fields we hear about advocacy and political sponsorship, but in information services, the ideas of advocacy for one's work and political sponsorship in the workplace have not been pursued. It was only when I was studying another area of information management that I realized that advocacy and advantageous political relationships could be useful to the information services manager. In an article written by Elizabeth Orna in 1978, it was suggested that in order to build an effective strategy for information services in an organization or community, the information providers, and certainly information managers, needed to know the organization well. Many people such as Helen Waldron, William S. O'Donnell, and a variety of others had written and continue to write about the value of 'knowing' the organization which the information service supports. So why was Orna's advice so different? For me, I think, it was the language she used.

According to Orna, this 'thorough knowledge' of the organization helps information services managers 'judge both the constraints and the opportunities' which apply to information services, 'and among the opportunities, whatever the form of the organization, is that of becoming skilled in making the organization work for us, and learning to play it as a responsive instrument' (Orna, 1978, p. 132). As one for whom musical interests have been important, I was pleased with Orna's simile, as I had been with Waldron's emphasis on 'harmonious' relationships within the organization (discussed in Chapter 6).

Orna's advice that information services professionals learn to 'play' the organization made sense to me, and the more I thought about it, and the more I observed those in the information services community whom I reckoned to be successful, the more it became very clear to me that, yes, success in information services management does come to those who know their parent organizations and communities well, but special success seems to come to those who know – and understand – how to 'play' their organizations for the advantage and support of the information services units for which they were responsible.

But how could that be, since (theoretically, at least) all information providers start with the same basic skills, the same basic resources, and, hopefully, the same basic training and education? It was only after much further observation that I came to realize what 'works' in information services: success (which we could define with Peter Drucker as 'effective' and 'efficient' information services) comes to those information services practitioners who have someone *else* in the organization or community who believe, with them, in the value of the information services and products they provide.

Defining information services

There is today a new understanding of what constitutes 'information services', and what is meant by 'information services management'. The terms are not new to the language, of course, but over the past few years, there has developed a concept of information, and of the provision of information, that now influences much of what is understood about the delivery of information services and products to those who need them. For one thing, the idea of 'information services' is being defined very broadly. As described in the *Introduction to the Series*, it is now recognized that the various constituent units of our society concerned with information have many of the same goals, objectives and, not surprisingly, many of the same concerns, including the practice of management. As a result, the jobs of those who provide information are being redefined, and broadened. In this new information workplace, anyone who is connected to information, who provides information in any form, is part of information services.

A logical and wise extension of this concept of information comes again from Elizabeth Orna, for in 1990 she wrote a very important book on managing information flow in organizations. Not limiting herself to traditional concepts and definitions of 'information', Orna pointed out that within the organization or enterprise, information will be found every-where, 'not just in formal repositories like libraries or information systems, and not just in those functions where people spend a lot of time reading, writing, or interacting with computers'. For Orna, the 'touchstone' (as she called it) for identifying information is simple: 'Is this something that people need to know and apply in their work, to achieve their, and the enterprise's objectives?' (Orna, 1990, p. 46). The list of items that meet Orna's criteria is long, and includes such things as customer records, financial records, internal information, external information, technical information, and information about the environment in which the enterprise operates. Significantly, for Orna's list, the 'form' in which the information is held is irrelevant, for information, in this context, is anything that the people who use the information services need to have. As information workers face the new millennium and a period in history when information as a commodity with tangible value will be organized, manip-ulated and disseminated in unheard-of and unthought-of ways, Orna's all-inclusive defnition makes much practical sense.

There are many component parts to this 'big picture' of information services, and although some workers in some of the specific sub-fields are occasionally uncomfortable with this 'umbrella' concept (as it has been called) of information services, most information workers are willing to accept that they are all part of a broader-based community of information services practitioners, whether they work in a traditional library or, at the other end of the spectrum, in a commercial information bureau. With this acceptance, it can be reasonably predicted that these same workers will turn to one another for further guidance, as they attempt to improve their productivity in the workplace. When they do so, they will find that many of their fears about mingling with other 'types' of information workers, their concerns about 'turf', are groundless.

For this book, there are a number of people who have been especially helpful to me, and I would like to acknowledge them. Andrew Berner, my business partner and friend, is consistent in his encouragement and support as I undertake new challenges, and I thank him for this encouragement and support. Without it I might not be able to do this work. Ann Lawes, with whom I developed many of these ideas as we organized our 'advocacy' seminars for TFPL Ltd., and Nigel Oxbrow, Managing Director of TFPL Ltd., both provide important stimulation for me in the exciting field of information services management, and I am very grateful for the good collegial relationship I have with them. David R. Bender, the Executive Director of the Special Libraries Association and a stimulating and provocative friend, continually challenges my thinking in these matters, and I am grateful to him for his wise counsel and friendship. Beth Duston, my strategic partner in many projects, offers on-going advice to me as I explore new ideas in the field, and I very much appreciate what she does for me. Of course my debt to Elizabeth Orna, whose influence on my work is described above, is great, and I commend her for her stimulating and original thinking in this complicated arena. Geraldine Turpie and Val Skelton at Bowker-Saur are literary colleagues *par excellence*, without whom I would not trust myself to write a word, and I thank them sincerely for their care and good counsel.

Guy St. Clair
New York
May 31, 1994

References

Orna, Elizabeth. 'Should we educate our users?' *Aslib Proceedings*. 30 (4), 1978.

Orna, Elizabeth. *Practical Information Policies: How to Manage Information Flow in Organizations*. Aldershot, England: Gower, 1990.

Chapter One

The value of advocacy and political sponsorship

Acquiring power and influence is necessary for the successful management of an information services department or unit, regardless of the nature of the community, parent organization, or other enterprise for which the department supplies information. In simplest terms, those who are responsible for providing information products and services cannot do so if they are not given the resources for providing those products and services. In today's competitive environment, resources are provided for those – including information services managers – who can demonstrate that the work they and their staff do is needed by the organization. To be able to demonstrate this value, information services managers must have power in the organization or community, and they must position themselves to influence others in the organization or community to support their work.

This concept is problematic for many in information services, simply because information and the components that make up information as a functional element in our society are assumed to be of little value (or are not thought of at all) except in terms of how they affect the resolution of some other problem, usually a problem not related to information as a specific subject. Most people do not sit down and say, in so many words, 'I think I'll think about information for a while'. For most people, except those involved in information services, concepts about information and the role of information in their lives are based solely on need: 'I must solve this problem. Where do I find the information that will enable me to do so?'. When the time comes to place a value on information or the information-gathering process most of these people do not even begin to think about information value in abstract terms. For them, information has value when they have a need for it, and when it can be produced to meet that need (or worse yet, for them, when it cannot be produced, which of course gives the required information even higher value). When they do not need information, members of the general public do not think about information, and in not thinking about it, of course, they put very little value on information.

On the other hand and in fact diametrically opposed to the public's point of view about the value of information, people who work with information and information services all the time tend, naturally enough, to place a very high value on information as an entity in and of itself. The classic story in this connection, told by one of the library profession's great storytellers, describes the university librarian (admittedly a product of an earlier generation of 'information workers', and certainly one who would never have thought of himself as an 'information services manager') who decried the emphasis on management concerns in library work with the statement that libraries are, in and of themselves, 'self-evidently good' (White, p. 123). Today, such a statement would not only be inaccurate, it would be a foolhardy admission of failure by an information services manager, librarian or otherwise, in understanding the role of library and information work in the organization or community to which the information services unit is attached. Even in the academic community, where some semblance of the 'ivory tower' convention continues to flourish despite the efforts of administrators and faculty 'management teams', much attention is being given to establishing the value of the academic libraries and to quantifying their roles in the education and research process. In other information settings as well, such information services departments as corporate archives, records management units, specialized libraries and the like are all being required to demonstrate value for the services and products they provide. Even directors and trustees in the public library community are now being asked by city managers, county supervisors and other administrative authorities to justify that the services they provide are in fact of value to the community, and these are services that until only recently were considered sacrosanct in those institutions. Library managers and other information services executives are being asked, by people who do not have their professional attachment to information, to explain why the services they provide should be supported.

Not that those who are asking the questions are doing so with malevolence, ill will, or any other evil intentions. In fact, in most cases, such requests for supporting documentation usually come with a well-phrased caveat, something along the lines of, 'I know and you know that the work you do is valuable, but in order to support it to the extent that you say you require, please tell us what you do and how your products and services affect our organization (or community or enterprise) as a whole'. W. Patrick Leonard, for example, an academic administrator in the United States, asked for new measures of effectiveness from his library staff. In a budget memorandum published as a model for other administrators (and which has been quoted in the book on customer services in this series), Leonard raised some very interesting and, for library managers in a traditional library setting, unusual points:

> I am going to ask you and your colleagues for a wholly new category of information to further justify your needs. As you probably know, 'outcome

assessment' has recently become a very popular concept in higher education. . . . At the risk of sounding faddish, I am going to ask you for information useful in outcome assessment - i.e., data that will more directly gauge the library's influence upon its various clients. Although the usual figures on collection size, circulation, and reference will continue to be of interest, they will no longer be sufficient. This information doesn't go far enough in a age concerned with the conflicting issues of quality and cost containment. . . .

I am looking for demonstrated relationships between library costs and benefits more closely related to the institution's teaching mission. . . . Is there a relationship between the nature of students' library use and their academic performance? . . . If we can isolate linkages between, for example, regular use of reference services and classroom performance or student retention then the library should be more competitive in the budget arena. If not, we may have to rethink the library's mission within the institution. (Leonard, p. 230-231)

For some information managers, of course, such direction is not a threat and is not seen as one. These people, working in organizations that require such justification in other departments and divisions, simply join in with the general effort and get on with the job. The difficulty comes, unfortunately, with those information services professionals who are not accustomed to placing a value on the work they do and who therefore must reconsider some of their own priorities in order to survive in the workplace.

The particular thesis of this book - that acquiring power and influence is necessary for the successful management of an information services organization - grows out of the recognition that a number of incorrect and perhaps awkward assumptions about information and the providing of information services and products are in place. In order to understand why information services professionals should be concerned with power and influence in the information workplace, these assumptions must be addressed and when necessary refuted, especially in light of the fact that modern information services and products, and the departments and units which provide them, have evolved from such a varied collection of institutional and organizational backgrounds. As a result of these diverse beginnings, conflicting and sometimes contradictory assumptions often lead to confusion, to misunderstanding and even, it has been known, to the establishment of counter-productive arrangements for the delivery of information services and products within the parent organization, the corporate entity or the community which supports the information services.

Among these assumptions, for example, is one which defines the information services department in terms of its place in the organization, positioning the provision of information as an overhead expense, as is done with accounting, human resources management, and some other functions in the organization. In these organizations, there is little correlation between the success of the organizational mission and the information provided by the information services department. The information services section of the organization is understood by senior management to be a non-income-producing department, a consumer of resources rather than a participant in the achievement of the organization's goals. An example might be a hospital library, seen within the hospital as a repository of books and journals, to be accessed when needed by the hospital staff, but organizationally classified as part of an administrative services department, whose overall manager supervises the housekeeping staff, the mail room and delivery functions, and the hospital security staff. This is obviously an inappropriate reporting structure for the staff of the library, since the hospital library, created as a research function, cannot possibly compete with the other departments of its group if the group manager is concerned with other such non-research, non-intellectually-based activities. In such an organization, the fact that the information services unit is wrongly positioned means that the value of the department has not been established (or has been wrongly established) and that efforts must be undertaken to raise the awareness of the decision makers in the organization about the work of the unit.

A second assumption has to do with a certain built-in inertia that comes when a work unit or entity already exists and has existed without question for some period of time. Most people who provide information do so in an information unit or organization that is already in place. At some point in time a decision was made to create the information unit, to provide information services and products for the enterprise, and since the department is already in place, its value is – ostensibly, at least – already in place as well. In many other organizations, the value of the information services unit is assumed, and little or no thought is given to defining that value, or enhancing it, either for the information stakeholders in the organization or for the decision makers who control the resources which support the department. In either case, when the products and services of the information services section are taken for granted, with few or no questions asked about the value of those products and services to the organization or community at large, it becomes easy to slip into a sort of organizational indifference about the information services unit.

Yet another assumption places the information services executives and their staff, the people who provide information services and products for the organization or community, in an 'outside' role. They are often not seen as 'part of the team', and because the work they do is so different from some other activities in the workplace, their information activities are seen as unusual and perhaps even a little mysterious. In these situations, information staff are often seen as somewhat aloof, and assumed to be uninterested in organization-wide activities. Senior managers and peers in the organization do not often ask the information staff to participate in committees and task forces created for special organizational projects, and the information people themselves, often thinking that the work they do is so 'different' that their efforts must be limited to that work, do not put themselves forward for organizational activities, which is a mistake.

Those who do not work with information often assume that the marketing of information services products and services is unnecessary, that when people need information, they will come to the particular information services unit, whether it is a library, records department, or any of the various others departments in an organization where information is collected, when they require the information. There is no need, according to this line of thinking, for information services to be marketed to constituent or even potential user groups. The archives section of a company, say, or the records section of a research institution exists as a repository for materials which are retained, for legal or historical purposes. The unit is already in place, it appears on the organization chart of the enterprise whose materials it contains, and everyone who is obligated to direct materials to the department knows to do so. But do others? Are there not employees in the organization, in public relations, perhaps, or in marketing, for whom some of the materials collected in the department could be useful? Would not a marketing effort, or at least an awareness-raising campaign, about the products and services of the department result in better use of the materials?

Related to this assumption of course is one which creates difficulties in many organizations, the idea that an information services unit and the people who work there do not need to be concerned with a proactive, customer-oriented perspective about their work. In the corporate and research environment, the need for on-going customer development effort is constant. No matter how sophisticated the employees of an organization are, there will always be those who will not think to call the information services staff when they are seeking additional documentation for a particular software program, or to take advantage of the organization's specialized library. For these people, if they think of these information services units at all, it is usually with the understanding that they are there for 'somebody else'. In every organization, there are always additional information services users who can be identified, and a proactive approach to information management can go far in dispelling the notion that information services are for a limited user base within the organization.

One of the most important assumptions that affects information services management, and how information services are supported in an organization, has to do with the actual work that information professionals do. This was starkly demonstrated in a study in 1987, in which the value of the information professional was recognized to be limited for a number of reasons, with one of the most important of these reasons being that 'the information professional's work – the creative activity that actually adds value to the otherwise inert material in the collection and makes it usable by and for clients – is unobservable mental work. Its invisibility to clients adds to its general lack of appreciation and low valuation.' (Veaner, p. [11]). Obviously, regardless of the kind of information products and services being offered, the unique and special training required for the development and delivery of those products and services is limited to the people who work there, and it would be a mistake to pretend otherwise. Users, peers, and management employees at all levels have no business interfering with or participating in any way in the day-to-day activities of an information services section, but the fact that they do not often leads to some confusion as to just what it is that information services professionals 'do'. There is a certain level of mystique about the work of an information services department, or a records management unit, or a specialized library, and because the lay person does not understand what it is that goes on there, he or she might be inclined to place a lower value on the products and services that are available there.

Another assumption which must be addressed, and which unfortunately affects all information services organizations in this day and age, is the uninformed notion that automation, in its myriad forms, brings information into an organization so quickly and so efficiently that staffing in information services departments can be reduced, often with some calculated formula that connects the cost of the information services labor force with the cost of the automation being considered. Many information services managers have been asked to justify the cost of this or that new system with the number of staff which can be eliminated. In fact, it is now clearly recognized in the information industry that automation does not necessarily lead to a reduction in the work force. What happens is that, with training and general support from the parent organization, the clever information services executive recognizes that he or she will be managing a department in which the productivity of the staff, the level of services performed, the quality of the products available for customers, and the contribution to the achievement of organizational goals will be seriously enhanced. The point of automation, if it needs to be made in this day and age, is simply that it enables the information worker to be more productive and the organization, particularly the information services department itself, to operate in a milieu that anticipates rather than reacts to the requirements of the organizational mission.

Whether information services practitioners accept these assumptions or not, it must be recognized that they affect information services and products as they are delivered in today's society, and certainly within the various environments in which information organizations are found. Such an assertion is based on the role of the information services professional, and how he or she is perceived in the organization, community or enterprise of which the information services department is a part. Perception plays a great role in every interaction in society, and no less so in the information interactions that take place in the workplace, the public library, the research or academic institution, or the school or other educational or training establishment. How people in these situations think about information and information services greatly affects their inclination to support or otherwise give attention to those services, and the wise information services executive recognizes, and accepts without rancor, that the perceptions of others about the work they and their staff do is part and parcel of the success (or lack of success) of the information services they are expected to manage. In recognizing the role that perceptions play in their success, information services managers position themselves to influence those perceptions for the good of the organization, community or enterprise which their information services units support (and not, coincidentally, for the good of the information units themselves).

Nevertheless, the effective information services executive, or even the information services provider (for those whose responsibilities do not embrace larger staffs and larger information services organizations), must not limit his or her concerns to perceptions alone. There are, in today's society, established conflicts about the delivery of information services and products which, if left unacknowledged, can seriously affect the ability of information services managers to achieve the objectives of the departments for which they are responsible. While all branches of information services are not equally affected by these (for want of a better term) disharmonies within information work, all information providers can benefit from recognizing that they exist and, if ignored, pose significant barriers to the effective delivery of information.

The first of these barriers has to do with stereotypes, and while this is not a book about the 'image' of the information worker, it must be conceded that stereotypes exist and must be dealt with. The difficulty comes with the assumption that information workers are alone in their concerns with stereotype and image. All professions fight this battle (the law, for example, or medicine, or even – and not surprisingly considering how far society has evolved in this respect during the last several decades – the clergy), and within the information services field, a wide range of stereotypes flourishes. Employees in the MIS department of every organization are assumed to be interested only in information technology, in the 'bells and whistles', and are chided for their lack of interest in customer service, user training, or the intellectual content that is provided through the technology. The organization's archivist is expected to be totally uninterested in the success of the enterprise at large, concerned only about having non-current materials securely stored and retrievable only through his or her intervention. Records management personnel, according to the common understanding, spend their days devising convoluted and arcane classification systems that obstruct rather than open up the records they manage, and, if the stereotype is to be believed, devise these systems so that they themselves provide the only approach mechanism through which the records can be accessed.

In the battle against stereotyping, of course, librarians are the information services practitioners who have the hardest job. Whether these information workers are employed in a public library, an academic institution, a school library or a specialized library in the corporate or research environment, the very word 'librarian' puts an immediate barrier between them and the people they must serve. Librarians are the victims of an ongoing conflict in society, a conflict that finds them and their professional colleagues straddling a major divide between absolute respect and admiration for the good work that they do and the excellence of the services that they provide (often under abominable conditions) and an equally absolute *lack* of respect because they are perceived, certainly unfairly, as being connected to an educational establishment that for a variety of reasons is discounted by most citizens and retreated from as soon as possible. For some reason, over the last fifty years or so, the 'idea' of 'librarianship' has moved, together with the 'idea' of 'teaching', into a realm of something very near disdain, wherein ordinary people, those not connected with either librarianship or teaching, seem to rebel or otherwise oppose the efforts of these people to be part of their lives.

On the other hand, these same people are not quite ready to 'turn against' librarianship and teaching, primarily because they recognize that even when librarianship and teaching do not come up to the standards that they are seeking (or that they imagine they are seeking), these two professions still remain a potent force in society. These people, the ordinary citizens of our society, are very quick to voice their support for libraries and education, declaring that they are important to society and vital to democracy. In fact, when it comes to pinning them down, most of these people are not really very interested in libraries and education. Speculations abound as to why this is so (e.g., people 'outgrow' their need for the structured approaches to learning that libraries and education offer, they prefer to do their own education and research, they are reluctant to seek guidance from someone else, etc.), but the reasons are in fact irrelevant. For many adults, much of what they *think* about libraries contradicts what they *say* they think about libraries, and therein lies the conflict for librarians as professionals in a society that tends to be, from time to time, only marginally tolerant of such intellectual activities as librarianship. As one observer of the library profession was said (perhaps apocryphally) to have remarked, 'People don't really like libraries, not as institutions. They just use them because they need to'. A harsh assessment, perhaps, but certainly one with some validity when librarians observe how they are treated in society.

The solution to this problem is simple. If the idea of 'librarian' and 'librarianship', by those names, has lost its value to society, as it has, but the functions of librarianship, (the organization of knowledge and the storage, retrieval and dissemination of knowledge, in whatever format) continue to be required by society at large, librarians – and to a lesser extent other information services workers as well – can take two steps to change things. First, they must stop calling themselves 'librarians'. The work they do and the value of that work are based on providing a commodity – information – that is needed by society. To be acknowledged for providing that commodity, librarians must somehow work into their 'label', this word they use to describe themselves, the concept that information, as a valued commodity, is part of what they do.

Second, librarians must reject absolutely and permanently their connection with education and the education establishment. Librarians and other information services workers exist to solve problems, to find for their users the information they need, and to provide that information in the products and services that best meet the requirements of the users. By characterizing themselves as members of the educational community, with their role being one of 'educating' users about how to find the information themselves, rather than as information providers who deliver the information to them, librarians perpetuate the unpleasant and 'schoolteacher-ish' role that much of society has come to expect of them, and which ultimately deprives them of their power to influence those in society who support their services.

What information services people are looking for, it seems, is to be taken seriously for the work they do, and the success of that quest is in their own hands, which is of course the point of this book. The picture described in the long digression above is quickly contrasted with another, one which at this point in time seems particularly pertinent. This is a picture of the information services worker as seen by Ann Lawes, a leader in the information services field who supervises training programs for information practitioners in the UK. In today's information workplace, the information employee expects to be taken seriously as an information provider and as a manager in the parent organization for which he or she provides information. In an interview, Lawes described that employee:

> An information manager has to be many things today. This person must be a team leader, a facilitator, must be able to monitor programs and evaluate programs and services, and must be willing to train. And at the same time, the manager is required to balance management skills, professional skills, and interpersonal skills. It's a tall order, but there's no choice, and today's information services organization requires a special kind of person, someone willing to bring these skills to the workplace.
>
> The hard part, of course, is what we've got to work around. Librarians and other information people have not, traditionally, been asked to do these things, to be these kinds of managers. And now they are. Information services management is no longer the place – if it ever was – for the loner lacking in inter-personal skills. It's too bad, but the bookish eccentric so beloved of our profession is out of place today, at least in information services management.
>
> People coming to us aren't looking for information that will enable them to deduce the answer. They want the answer, and they don't care where it comes from, as long as it is timely and accurate. Nowadays, our users are looking for

a one-stop shop, for both internal and external information, and if we have to refer them somewhere else, we will, but that's not what they want. They want to come to us for the answer. And the manager of the information unit must recognize and understand that. (Lawes, p. 4)

There is nothing inherently *wrong* about either of these two perspectives on information services work, but the fact of the matter is that information services are supported, with appropriate resources provided, to the extent that those who observe information services understand the value of those services. Value, for those not involved in the management of information services, is related not only to the value of the information services and products themselves but to their own perceptions about the practitioners who provide those products and services.

With information services, there is a direct correlation in how these services are supported, a correlation based not so much on what these perceptions *should* be, but on what the perceptions *are*. For the manager of the information services unit, the trick is to change the invalid perceptions, to make them match reality, and this is done through the effective use of advocates and political sponsors for the work of the library, records department, management information system MIS group, or whatever other information services unit is producing information services and products for the organization, community or enterprise.

Within this context, advocacy and political sponsorship can be defined as those efforts, taken by the information services practitioners in an organization, community, or enterprise, to encourage others to support the work of the information services department and, at the same time, to encourage those people to develop relationships which can have a positive influence in the decision making process for allocating resources for the funding of information services.

For there to be an ambiance in which the information services practitioner and/or manager can identify these advocates and political sponsors, in order to encourage them to support the work of the information services department, there are two steps which can be taken. The first, of course, has to do with affecting the perceptions of others about information services, and the value of information services to the organization or community for which the services are provided.

Secondly, stereotypes about information delivery must be ignored publicly and, within the boundaries of the department itself, attacked vociferously, with each member of the information services staff avoiding, whenever possible, any temptation to fall into stereotypical behavior. At the same time, all staff must acknowledge that stereotypical barriers to effective information delivery are already in place, and these barriers must be dismantled, with the staff working doubly hard in order to prevent establishing its own barriers, based on its own stereotypes about information and information services. When these steps are taken, the information services manager is ready to look at advocacy and political sponsorship as funda-mental elements in the successful achievement of the department's – and the organization's – goals. He or she can then determine how advocates and political sponsors can be used to enhance the role of the information services operation within the organization, with the happy result that support for the department, both appropriate financial resources and encouragement of the more general sort, will be realized.

References

Lawes, Ann. 'What's expected of an information services executive?' *InfoManage: The International Management Newsletter for the Information Services Executive*. June, 1993 [Prototype Issue].

Leonard, W. Patrick. 'This year is different: Facing outcome assessment.' *The Journal of Academic Librarianship*. 18, September, 1992.

Veaner, Allen B. 'Introduction.' *President's Task Force on the Value of the Information Professional/Final Report/Preliminary Study*. Washington, DC: Special Libraries Association, 1987.

White, Herbert S. 'Management: A strategy for change.' *Canadian Library Journal*, October, 1978, reprinted in White, Herbert S. *Librarians and the Awakening From Innocence: A Collection of Papers*. Boston, MA: G.K. Hall and Company, 1989.

Chapter Two

Corporate culture: its influence on information services

Much has been written about corporate culture in the business community, but except for an occasional article in the professional journals, little attention has been given to the importance of corporate or organizational culture in the information environment. In fact, if the pursuit of power and influence is accepted as an appropriate component in the successful management of an information services operation, and if in that pursuit advocacy and political sponsorship are incorporated into the managerial process, certainly a recognition of the influence of an organizational culture will provide useful direction for the information services manager.

In the business community, organizational culture (usually referred to as 'corporate' culture), is recognized for what it is, a certain intangible quality about the organization, perhaps an informal (or in some cases, a formal) style, a certain character or organizational 'personality', or way of doing things. Organizational culture has been variously defined, but generally an understanding of organizational culture has much to do with expectations within the organization or the corporation:

> ... A set of expected behaviors that are generally supported within the group ... unwritten 'rules' that have an immense impact on behavior ... [and] which affect every aspect of organizational functioning. (Silverzweig and Allen, p. 33)

The reference to 'impact' is important, for in fact this unseen culture, this intangible way of looking at things, is very powerful and can have a significant influence on whether or not the objectives of the organization – and the subunits that make up the organization – succeed or fail. For an information services manager in a publishing organization, for example, the design and dissemination of information products and services will be greatly affected by the 'tone' of the company. If the senior officers in the company see it as an old-line, well-established business, as carrying on a long tradition of literary publishing with profits coming from the steady sales of books and journals of a type already known to be successful in the marketplace, the level of information services will be similarly characterized. Records management, for one, will be organized along traditional functions, with commissioning, editorial, marketing, sales and financial records generally spread throughout the organization by department. When it is necessary to determine from one or another department some piece of information that might affect another department's work, much time and energy will be devoted to gathering the information, with all interested parties recognizing that the *process* of gathering information is time-consuming. While there may be some frustration from one or another of the people involved, such frustration is accepted as being built into the way work is organized in the company. There is not a great deal of concern, and certainly not on the part of senior management, since profits remain steady and the question of efficiency or lack of efficiency in records management has never been recognized as a component in the profits the company realizes from the sale of its literary products.

On the other hand, the management of a more venturesome publishing firm seeking to broaden its product line might spend a considerable portion of its resources in automating as completely as possible the records management function, preferring to use its human resources for researching new product opportunities and new markets for its various products. In such an environment, the information services manager and his or her staff will not hesitate to take a proactive approach, perhaps even going so far as to recommend newer and less traditional applications for its records management system and integrating such functions as company archives, financial reporting and the like with functions already automated.

The difference between the two companies, it can be agreed, is indeed one of corporate culture. In the first (admittedly an extreme example, but not an unusual one in the publishing industry), the attitude already in place is a culture of comfort: 'We're doing things well enough to suit us. We bring in a profit and our workers are satisfied'. The 'expected behaviors' (in Silverzweig and Allen's term) is one of acceptance, of recognizing that in this company the efforts of the employees are those that keep the company mildly successful. Nothing more is expected or desired.

In the second company, all staff look for opportunities to *increase* profits, not just in sales but in organizational efficiency as well. It's an ambiance that tolerates and probably even encourages a certain level of maverick thinking in its employees. The information services staff, recognizing this, loosens its creative thinking on a plan for integrating all of the organization's information activities and even though the staff will come up with some processes and procedures that might fail, it will also, in such a milieu, create processes that will bring about greater productivity and better efficiency in the work that is its responsibility. In this company, creativity is an 'expected behavior'.

Most of those who study organizational culture as a specific phenomenon of organizational behavior recognize that the basic emphasis has to do with shared experiences and values, that the influence of the culture on the individual relates directly to his 'buying into' or participating in, in some way, the organizational culture. Terence Deal and Allan Kennedy use this concept in their comments about the 'business of culture', which they connect to the success or lack of success in the organization. 'Successful companies' they suggest, 'emphasize shared values that define the character of the organization' (Deal and Kennedy, p. 47).

Ralph Kilmann, too, emphasizes the cooperative and sharing aspect of organizational culture, which he defines as:

> Shared values, beliefs, expectations, norms and assumptions that give [the organization] a flavor. What is meant by 'shared' is that the people of the group or the whole company essentially have the same set of values, expectations, norms; it is not of one person. It must be shared as part of a larger community. (Kilmann, p. 164)

Certainly such shared values and expectations are evident in the information services functions of some of the electronic manufacturers in America today. A visit to the campus-like facilities of some of these companies can be surprising. Located in remote settings with towering mountains in the distance, with elaborate sports facilities at hand and jogging trails outlining the perimeter of the grounds, the physical arrangement of the place gives the impression of a manufacturing ambiance that encourages creative productivity. Certainly in such an environment those responsible for information management recognize that the sharing of information is beneficial to the company as a whole, regardless of whether the information consists of research support, corporate management information, or marketing and sales information. Indeed, in such an environment, any attempts to establish information 'turf' or personal information fiefdoms would be quickly met with disdain and disfavor, since sharing in the work of the organization as a whole, the 'community' Kilmann refers to, is required for success in the company.

Sometimes, of course, the culture has evolved on its own, without the direction or motivation of any specific person or group of people, a pattern recognized by Edgar Schein when he identified organizational culture as a set of 'basic assumptions'. These assumptions have developed, Schein suggests:

> To cope with problems of external adaptation and internal integration, [and the pattern] has worked well enough to be considered valid and to be taught to new members as a correct way to perceive, think and feel in relation to those problems. (Schein, p. 67)

In the more traditional of the two publishing firms described earlier, the validity of the 'basic assumptions' has been established through the continuation of the profit cycle and the satisfactions of senior management and the people who work there, and such satisfactions must, of course, be recognized. After all, every person (and every company) does not expect to be a trend-setter, and there are many people who are distinctly uncomfortable when they find themselves expected to perform in a manner that runs counter to their own values and their own expectations of themselves. The librarian in that publishing firm, for example, may very well have been drawn to librarianship and to the publishing industry because he or she wanted a career in an intellectual and (supposedly) non-threatening environment. By finding employment in an organizationally conservative firm, that person's professional and personal values have been matched with an atmosphere that is rewarding and fulfilling. As long as the company is satisfied and the employee is satisfied, all else is irrelevant.

In considering the influence of an organizational culture within the various component subunits that make up the organization, the qualities of the organizational culture are not necessarily positive. Deal and Kennedy go even further than the concept of 'basic assumptions' in their analysis of the development of an organizational culture, and they assign to it very specific characteristics in terms of information flow within the organization. For them, organizational or corporate culture is:

> A hidden hierarchy through which information flows. . . . The cultural network of spies, storytellers, priests, whisperers, cabals, that provide the primary means of communication within the organization, that not only transmits information but also interprets the significance . . . without respect to position or titles. It is an informal yet complex grapevine that carries values and culture across levels and divisions and among people. (Deal and Kennedy, p. 54)

Such a negative 'spin' to the concept of organizational culture can be pretty devastating when the information services executive takes a look at his or her organization and attempts to relate the conduct of this 'hidden hierarchy' to the delivery of information products and services. Certainly there are those types of communities, organizations and enterprises that lend themselves to such petty activities, but one would like to think that the achievement of departmental or organizational goals would take precedence – by a long shot – over any advantages that might be realized from participating in such a network.

In the first place, most employees and most 'groups' of employees within an organization acknowledge, either overtly or privately, a certain level of loyalty to the organization, or at least to the 'idea' of the organization. 'Since we are social beings,' writes Gordon F. Shea on the subject of company loyalty, 'we are bound both to acquire loyalties and to be dependent on them. It is difficult for us to live together in an organized fashion without loyalties, for they allow us to be confident of some people and things so that we can get on to focusing our attention and efforts on other things' (Shea,

p. 17). That confidence plays an important role in the success of organizations – and departments within organizations, such as information services
units – in achieving their goals and objectives. Information employees
who are confident in their place in the organization and in the value of their
contributions to the organization can, as Shea states, 'get on' with the
creative work of providing those information products and services that
best meet the needs of the members of the organization who come to them
for information. The presence of that organizational loyalty will of necessity
diminish the negative influences of the 'cultural network' Deal and Kennedy
allude to, simply because those influences would contradict the efforts
of the employees in succeeding at what they have to do.

At the same time, accepted notions of human behavior come into consideration here, and characterizing the 'cultural network' as a conglomeration
of negative influences is counter to most people's views of themselves and
the roles they play in an organization or community. Altruistic motivations
aside, anyone who must work with others – despite the fleeting pleasures
of temporary little 'power plays' – cannot run the risk of being known as a
spy, storyteller (in the negative sense) or whisperer. Those people soon
learn that to advance within a company or organization, a reputation as a
naysayer or defeatist is a barrier not easily overcome. The information
employee who 'transmits information' about, say, the failure of a researcher
from the packaging department to find a particular piece of information,
or about the cost of delivering that information, and who then 'interprets
the significance' of what he or she is transmitting will soon have a bad
reputation within the organization (to leave aside any discussion of the
ethical issues involved). Not only will that employee no longer be trusted
to advise researchers about their information needs, he or she is likely
eventually to be found looking for a job. Such a scenario is highly unlikely,
or *should* be so, in a well-managed information operation. The achievement
of the objectives of the department must – and will in due course – far
outweigh such smallness of thinking on the part of individual information
staff members.

In the present context, the term 'corporate culture' is adapted from the
business community and is preferred to 'organizational' culture, not because
what is written here is limited to information services units within the
business community, but because 'corporate' as a descriptor seems to refer
more inclusively to the people who make up the overall group. Thus for our
purposes the word is used in the classical sense, not to allude specifically
to the business community but to any 'corporate' entity or organization
in which the library, records management unit or other information services
department is located.

In attempting to establish a connection between the information environment and the parent organization, and how the corporate culture of the
parent organization affects the delivery of information products and services,
the information services manager can perform a very simple test. It was

outlined by John Kok in a now classic essay, and its basic idea has to do with determining the organization's attitude about information. In fact, as Kok stated it, 'no single factor has greater influence on the library manager than the organization's attitude toward information' (Kok, p. 524). It is up to the information services manager to carry out, usually informally, an information 'attitude audit' within the company, community or other enterprise which the information services unit supports, in order to determine which characteristics within the organization can be adapted to match those of the information services unit, and, of course, which to recognize and avoid.

An information 'attitude audit' might look at such things as how information is used in the community or organization, what role information plays in the successful achievement of organizational goals, how individual people move information around (particularly decision makers within the organization and the various subunits and their reporting structures), the formats they use, the role of personal information procurement in the different management levels of the organization, the interest in end-user information procurement, and similar considerations related to the delivery of information throughout the organization. Certainly any such data gathering, whether informal or formal, would begin with a look at how people in the organization feel about information. Is their work information intensive? Do they require information to do their work, or is their work primarily based on continuous and/or routine processing of materials and functions brought to them by others? Are they expected to use information in the work they do, and if so, is the organization (to portray the situation perhaps too simplistically) 'old-fashioned', 'traditional', 'status quo', 'modern' or even 'avant garde' in its culture? And how does that characterization affect information and the flow of information in the organization?

Related to such an 'attitude audit' and providing equally useful direction is an exercise which Elizabeth Orna calls 'an audit of human resources in relation to information activities'. This audit seeks the participation – at all levels within the enterprise – of not only the people who *provide* the information, but the users of information as well. The purpose of the audit is to determine how effectively the people who are asked 'are contributing to the enterprise's information', but what is interesting about Orna's list is that these questions, when asked of these people, can also be useful in helping to determine the organizational 'attitude' about information, a necessary preliminary step prior to analyzing actual information needs and organizing the resources for meeting those needs.

Orna's 'human resources/information activities' audit asks of these employees, both information providers and information customers, such questions as:

> Is the nature of their information activities appropriate for their role in the enterprise?

Is the level at which they are engaged in information activities appropriate for the level of their job?

Do they receive from other people the information which they need?

Do they communicate information to all the other people who need it for their work?

Are their qualifications, experience, skills and knowledge being appropriately used in their information activities?

Have they potential for further development which would allow them to contribute more fully to the objectives of the information policy?

Do they receive appropriate help from the information technology in use? (Orna, pp. 85–89)

A single example can serve to illustrate the value of the 'attitude audit' and give the information services manager a useful profile for the delivery of information products and services. In a well-known professional association, with members who are writers and scientists in archaeology, history and anthropology, the special library serving their information needs offers only limited services. There is no access to the Internet, even for electronic mail, so the members, all of whom have such access in their own offices (usually through academic or other research institutions), cannot connect with their organization's library and must physically come to the library to use it. When there, because of limited staff, users must find the materials they need for themselves, they must do their own photocopying, and when they are seeking guidance in searching for this or that piece of information, the information interview with the library staff member is perfunctory, hurried and often results in the user's information need being only partially met. The 'attitude' of the organization is clear: information is available for those who know how to find it. For the members of the association, the nature of their information activities is *not* appropriate for their role in the organization and certainly the level of their information work is not appropriate to that role. These members should not be spending their time looking for information, except for those situations when they choose to engage in 'browsing and serendipity' (as one observer characterized such information searching). These writers and scientists should be able to send e-mail messages through to the association's library and the library staff should find the information for them. By asking pertinent questions about information use within the organization and the levels of the various information activities in which the users and the information staff are involved, the organization's information services management can deduce quite readily the association's attitude about information, and of course react accordingly.

The gathering together of these various 'pictures', as it were, of information attitudes throughout the organization will enable the information services executive to piece together a composite profile of the corporate culture with respect to information and the information products and services for which the manager and his or her staff are responsible. Of course it can only be a composite profile, for regardless of how small the organization is (even the smallest law firm, for example, with only one or two partners), the person responsible for the management of information services will discover that different people, different sections and departments, and, indeed, different personnel and management levels will have vastly different ideas about information and its role in their work and in the success of the organization itself. Regardless of the nature of the information services, whether they encompass internal records, external research materials, or some combination of both, attitudes about information will vary throughout the organization. Even the example above is a vast oversimplification, for while some of the writers and scientists have reached the point in their careers where information should be brought to them, others will, indeed, prefer, to do their own research, even the most laborious research, and no matter how willing or available the information staff is, these people will not use their services beyond very basic levels. Such varying attitudes will have to be taken into consideration, with cooperative and conflicting values weighed against one another, before the information services manager can successfully integrate this information into the information services management process for the organization.

Nevertheless, when the information services manager has begun to pull the results of his or her 'attitude audit' into place (and it will be only a beginning, for the audit itself, being informal, is ongoing), the information services staff can begin to think about how the information products and services for which they are responsible can be designed to meet the needs of the information customers. It was Marlene Vogelsang who, in 1989, first identified the relationship between corporate culture and quality information services as a management tool:

> Understanding the role and influence of corporate culture can be a valuable technique in the management of a library or information center. The prevailing culture is a reflection of the parent organization that has an impact both directly and indirectly on all departments or divisions. (Vogelsang, p. 16)

How that 'reflection' affects information delivery can be best demonstrated by looking at how the information staff connects with the organization and other employees within the organization. Think about a government agency, for example, that supplies information and direction for a specific group of citizens who call the department for advice. If it is a department in which the work of the department is viewed by staff as of relatively limited or unessential value to the larger community, that viewpoint is going to be mirrored throughout the agency. If, additionally, the department has an organizational 'attitude' about information that views it as a 'bother', as 'getting in the way' of the real work of the agency, that position is going to prevail throughout the agency and of course will affect the delivery of information by those workers whose responsibility it is to provide the information. Such inconveniences to information customers as unanswered telephone calls, or telephones not answered until they have rung twenty or thirty times, or customers being put on an interminable 'hold', or hours of service that reflect staff working hours but ignore customers' service preference, all are 'reflections', as Vogelsang refers to them, of a corporate culture that affects service.

Imagine, though, another government agency in which senior management has determined that citizens' requests will be given priority. Management has been able to obtain resources for funding the systems and personnel required for such a level of service, and the overall attitude within the department is one of proactive, intensively determined 'customer service'. Certainly such an attitude prevails in the information services units of the department as well, since any deviation from such well-defined corporate culture would impede the successful achievement of the department's mission, as determined by senior management. In this agency, the telephones are programmed to offer a useful recorded message if not answered by an agency employee by the second ring, no caller is ever put through to more than one person before his or her query is considered, and special staff are recruited to handle calls outside normal business hours in the community where the agency is located, since many enquiries come in from citizens living in different time zones.

Thus in every organization, corporate culture operates on two levels, both on the organizational level and within the various departments and subunits which make up the organization as a whole. Even when the departmental 'culture' has not been specifically identified or recognized, it can be established and developed. Judy Labovitz, in speaking of a specialized library in the corporate setting, has pointed out that not only does each company or organization have a corporate 'personality' or culture, as discussed here, but that '. . . one really needs to develop a library culture. This library culture should develop naturally out of the service philosophy and the energy and personalities of the people who work in the library.' (Labovitz, p. 8). Surely Labovitz's concept can be applied across the entire information spectrum? If, for example, within a hospital's patient records department the 'caring' concepts from the hospital's overall mission statement are incorporated into the work of the department and if, as part of their efforts to match their department's mission with that of the parent organization, the management of the patient records department has established certain accuracy or speed of delivery standards for the department, the inclusion of those standards (and the acceptance of them by all employees involved in the delivery of patient records) can lay the foundation for a departmental 'culture' that effectively determines how well the department does or does not function.

Vogelsang recognizes that it is '. . . the shared values and assumptions of the employees that underline culture . . . give it strength and power. Acknowledging culture acknowledges the importance and value of people in the organization.' (Vogelsang, p. 17). In the example just cited, of course, management personnel in the patient records section of the hospital would be poor managers indeed if they did not bring other staff into the design of those accuracy and speed of delivery standards mentioned. Obviously management support and enthusiasm are vital to the acceptance of any organizational initiative, but in this case, that support and enthusiasm must underscore the staff's own enthusiasm for such standards. In working together to establish the standards and in connecting the establishment of the standards to the hospital's overall mission, the information services staff, in this case those who deliver patient information, and management have developed that departmental 'culture' that Labovitz suggests and recommends.

Such departmental culture cannot, of course, stand alone, and for an information services unit to succeed, its personnel must tap into the shared values within the organization. If the staff who work in the patient records department of that hospital are not interested in the overall mission of the parent organization, there is little chance that senior management's enthusiasm for more accurate or faster delivery of information will have any effect on the performance of the staff. No employees, regardless of whether they are involved in information services or perform some other function within the organization, can be expected to perform well unless they understand the relationship between what they do and the objectives of the company or organization as a whole. Thus information services managers in the hospital must devote some time and attention to ensuring that their staff members understand their role at the hospital, how their work affects the level of service offered to the patients who use the hospital's services, and how, ultimately, the hospital's success in achieving its mission is directly related to how well these information delivery personnel do their work.

There are a variety of techniques through which managers can relate the work of the information services staff to the overall mission of the organization, but how does that staff become part of the 'cultural network' within the organization? Obviously the usual activities are valuable, such things as knowing who is doing what research in the organization, or recognizing certain patterns of activity through the implementation of the SDI service. Beyond these, however, other steps can be taken which can assure a tangible level of activity between information services staff and others in the parent organization. Two of the most successful are the establishment of ongoing working relationships related to specific activities within the organization and participation in project teams.

Think about the work that is done by, say, the Vice-President for Corporate Relations at a major magazine publisher. Part of this senior manager's work has to do with ongoing corporate issues, but on an annual basis, he and his staff are responsible for generating the company's annual report, a glossy forty or fifty page document with not only the usual report-type information, but many handsome photographs, special text blocks, charts, and similar 'glamorous' information intended to convey how well the company is succeeding at accomplishing its mission. For this Vice-President, his most trusted ally throughout the year is a specially designated member of the magazine's editorial library, who as part of his assignment is expected to track ideas, issues and other salient subjects as they come up throughout the year, towards the end of having available, for the Vice-President of Corporate Relations, whatever material he might need for the compilation of the magazine's annual report. The library employee, while carrying out his usual work within the editorial library, becomes by nature of this ongoing 'special' assignment the organization's *de facto* corporate historian. At the same time, he becomes an ideal conduit into the editorial library for information about issues that are of concern to the organization as a whole. As such, he is not only working as part of the corporate culture himself, he is in a position to participate in the development of that culture within the organization, a role that gives him and the editorial library no small significance in the overall functional order of the organization.

Information services employees can also tap into the corporate culture through participation in project teams. While some employees might resist such assignments (because of a perceived increased workload, for example, or some political concern, resulting in a lack of interest in working with the group), they can be extremely beneficial for the information services department or unit within the organization. In the first place, information services employees know better than anyone else in the organization how information is obtained, how it is delivered, and how it is used, so a staff member from an information services unit is a primary candidate to be the information 'point-person' for the project team. More important, however, is the opportunity such participation provides for learning more about the parent organization as a whole, for becoming more visible within the company or organization, and for having a direct influence on decisions that are being made that can affect not only the information services unit which the employee represents but the overall organization as well.

Think about, for example, a manufacturing plant for which senior management and employees have been interested, for some time, in organizing a child-care center for employees' children. So far the idea has been only a concept, but now there is pressure from one of the employee unions to address the subject seriously. Since contract negotiations will be coming up in eighteen months or so, management has decided to put together a committee to do a feasibility study about the possibility of such a child-care center. The manager of the plant's technical library has been asked to serve on the committee, and while she herself has little personal interest in the child-care center (her children are adults now), she recognizes that this is a subject which needs to be addressed at the plant.

By accepting a position on the committee, she becomes the information resource for its work and, at the same time, puts herself in deliberate contact with a variety of fellow employees, many of whom might never have any reason to use the technical library. By doing so, she is able to get a 'feel' for the culture of the company as it affects information and her and her staff's delivery of information, and by using the committee as a mechanism for gathering information that will be of use to her and her staff, her contribution to the work of the committee is, on a larger scale, made more valuable.

The interesting thing about corporate culture is that it exists, everyone connected with the organization knows it exists (even if they do not recognize that they know it), and they all buy into it. It should be evident that such a happy situation can lead to tremendous advocacy opportunities for those who are responsible for information services, those who are, in fact, the knowledge workers in societies, the information services practitioners. Peter Drucker adroitly summed up the situation for information workers in his book on the post-capitalist society, in which he advanced the idea that educated people (and, it might be inferred, those responsible for maintaining the very records, artefacts and information that contribute to education), are a new, and different, class of people:

> In all earlier societies, the educated person was an ornament. He or she embodied *Kultur* – the German term which in its mixture of awe and derision is untranslatable into English (even 'highbrow' does not come close). But in the knowledge society, the educated person is society's emblem; society's symbol; society's standardbearer. The educated person is the social 'archetype', to use the sociologist's term. He or she defines society's performance capacity. But he or she also embodies society's values, beliefs, commitments. If the feudal knight was the clearest embodiment of society in the early Middle Ages, and the 'bourgeois' under Capitalism, the educated person will represent society in the post-capitalist society in which knowledge has become the central resource.
>
> This must change the very meaning of 'educated person'. It must change the very meaning of what it means to be educated. It will thus predictably make the definition of an 'educated person' a crucial issue. With knowledge becoming the key resource, the educated person faces new demands, new challenges, new responsibilities. *The educated person now matters.* (Drucker, pp. 210-211)

If those responsible for managing and providing information for any organization, corporation, or community will allow themselves, this new way of looking at knowledge and education can be their means for finding a wide-ranging panoply of support for the work they do. As senior management and the information customers who use their services become more and more convinced of the value of knowledge and education in the successful achievement of their organizational or community goals, the information services workers will find their roles becoming increasingly valuable and increasingly recognized. These information 'navigators', like the librarians of old who knew how to lead the way to information, can become a senior manager's or an information user's most valuable colleague in the community. When that happens, it is up to the information services manager to recognize just what these senior managers and these information customers can do for information services. These are people who respect what information professionals do with information, and it is up to the information professionals to determine how to take advantage of this new support and this new understanding of the role they play in the organization, corporation or community. Suddenly, the entire equation is turned around, and instead of information people going 'hat in hand' to the decision makers in the organization to request resources to do the work they must do, they now find themselves being courted by the information stakeholders to tell them – the stakeholders – what information services staff need in order to provide the best information and how to find those resources. It comes with the recognition that information services are, in simplest terms, those services that enable information users to acquire the knowledge they need, to do the work they need to do. The corporate culture is changing, and with that change comes an amazing opportunity for information services professionals to play a leading role in the success of the parent organization or community where they work.

There might be, of course, a more cynical side to this picture. It is possible that today's particular interest in corporate culture is not so much from some inborn or altruistic interest in making things better, but because it is one path for addressing the increasing demand of customers for quality in the work that is done for them. There are undoubtedly as many cries for quality in information delivery as in all other aspects of modern life, but the lack of quality in information services is no more or no less than anywhere else. Yes, we hear about numbers of queries being answered incorrectly, or incompletely, but there are obviously as many (if not more) queries that are answered correctly. Otherwise, financially aware institutions would not permit the information services departments to continue, and in those institutions where finances are not a concern, other influences would force the provision of quality information. So we do not necessarily connect the modern interest in corporate culture to the quest for quality, although that plays a part, but we can see it as a newer, healthier approach to doing better, more productive, and more effective work in the environment in which we choose to work. For information services professionals, that means recognizing that corporate culture affects the way information is delivered.

References

Deal, Terence, and Kennedy, Allan. *Corporate Culture: The Rites and Rituals of Corporate Life.* Boston, MA: Addison-Wesley, 1982.

Drucker, Peter F. *Post-Capitalist Society.* New York: HarperCollins, 1993.

Kilmann, Ralph M. *Managing Beyond the Quick Fix.* San Francisco: Jossey-Bass, 1989.

Kok, John. 'Now that I'm in charge, what do I do?' *Special Libraries.* 71 (12), December, 1980.

Labovitz, Judy. 'Managing a special library.' *Journal of Library Administration.* 6 (3), Fall, 1985.

Orna, Elizabeth. *Practical Information Policies: How to Manage Information Flow in Organizations.* Aldershot, England: Gower, 1990.

Shea, Gordon F. *Company Loyalty: Earning It, Keeping It.* New York: American Management Association, 1987.

Schein, Edgar. *Organizational Culture and Leadership: A Dynamic View.* San Francisco and London: Jossey-Bass, 1985.

Silverzweig, Stan, and Allen, Robert. 'Changing the corporate culture.' *Sloan Management Review.* 17 (3), Spring, 1976.

Vogelsang, Marlene. 'The reflection of corporate culture in the library or information center.' *Library Management Quarterly.* 12 (2), Spring, 1989.

Chapter Three
The benefits of cooperation

It might seem slightly incongruous to discuss cooperation in a book about the role of power and influence in the management of information services, but in fact, for most information services professionals, cooperation is an integral part of successful information delivery. The information transaction has traditionally been based upon cooperative effort, and the activity through which an information seeker approaches an information provider and acquires the information he or she is seeking will, more often than not, include some form of cooperative exchange before the information transaction is concluded. All information providers at one time or another turn to colleagues, either within the organization or community, or separate from it, for advice, guidance, further refinement of the enquiry, and similar exchanges which enable the provider to augment or expand his or her own capacity for providing the information.

The achievement of success in each information interaction is of course the goal of every information services manager, and the extent to which he or she is able to incorporate cooperative practices into the efforts of the information services staff plays a large role in determining the success or failure of the information services program in the organization or community.

Information services practitioners have traditionally utilized cooperation; it is part of the idea. Certainly librarians and library managers, with their organized interlibrary loan programs, consortia, and other cooperative and networking arrangements have long relied on formal cooperation as a mechanism for enabling them to provide the materials their users seek. In fact, without such programs, many libraries could not service their users' needs, as is attested to frequently within the profession as librarians and library managers discuss the imbalances that come up regularly between the large libraries, which are most frequently the suppliers of materials, and the small libraries, which are the borrowers.

In that branch of information services generally referred to as 'specialized' librarianship, wherein information and information materials are supplied (as Wilfred Ashworth has described specialized libraries) for the exclusive use and 'private advantage' of the organization which provides financial support for the library, cooperation has long been identified as a basic characteristic of the service (Ashworth, p. 6). Many authors and teachers have remarked on this special quality in specialized librarianship, with J. Burkett's statement being typical:

> That no library and information service can be self-sufficient, but needs to become involved in the exploitation of shared resources, has been an established fact since the early 1930s. (Burkett, p. 377)

And although writing in 1971 and in language that seems a little dated today, Helen J. Waldron made a very clear case for interpersonal cooperation and the role it plays in specialized libraries and information centers:

> ... Another major difference between special libraries and others is their marked dependence on other libraries for materials and even for reference help. No special library, no matter how restrictive the subject area or field in which it is working, can hope to have an exhaustive collection. It has neither the need nor the desire to compete with the academic libraries which attempt ever more zealously, it seems, to cover exhaustively all materials in not just one, but several fields. Special libraries, for one thing, are seldom favored by generous space allocations in which to collect and store. Instead they are expected to supply carefully tailored information *when* it is needed to the person who needs it. In order to meet this goal, and still work within the constraints of space and collection limitations, special librarians over the years have built up an informal network of personal associations. Some of this is achieved through professional organizations, and there are many of them. ... Indeed, their principle value to many of their members seems to be that they provide an opportunity - in both geographic and subject units - for personal contact and unofficial arrangements between libraries. (Waldron, p. 65)

Indeed, whether those contacts evolve, as Waldron suggested, from memberships and activities in professional associations or from some other source, they are, in fact, a vital component of successful work in the specialized library community. So much so that Andrew Ettinger, in a presentation about the value of information, included 'networked contacts (both external and internal)' as one of several 'principles' of successful information services management (Ettinger, p. 3). Unfortunately, the very concept of networking, as an activity in society as a whole, has been much discussed, argued about and even trivialized, but like much that is so treated, the basic concept is a good one and one that, when applied appropriately in a professional context, can provide tangible and frequently measurable rewards. The concept that Ettinger - along with many others - puts forth has much value in library and information services work and is certainly a useful component in the cooperative process.

Much of this cooperation has to do, of course, with the procurement of *external* information for the users of the specialized library or information center, which is why such cooperative endeavors can be successful in library work. It is worth considering, however, whether such cooperation can be viable for other types of information services. These same techniques (interlibrary loans, consortia, contractual networks, etc.) are not necessarily available in other types of information services, primarily because these units are usually working exclusively with internal information, or some version of information access that combines internal and external information. Yet when connected to such pursuits, the basic concepts of networking and cooperation can take on a slightly different focus and can, in fact, be applied to other types of information services work. Such practices, now common, as the establishment of user groups within a company or organization for people who work with certain specific computer programs, or certain types of hardware, represent an accepted and productive cooperative endeavor for these employees. Such cooperation naturally benefits the employee and enables him or her to feel more comfortable about using these tools, but at the same time, the employee's productivity and level of commitment to the work that he or she is responsible for is also heightened. Despite the fact that such user groups do not necessarily, as a group, share the specifics of each other's work (and, in fact, if the user group includes an external network as well as an internal one, it is frequently forbidden for such employees to do so), the informal training and professional growth that these people acquire, coupled with their increasing comfort with the activity, increases their value as employees.

There are several cooperative activities which lend themselves to all information services work, regardless of whether the work is in a specialized library or information center, in a corporate archives, in an MIS department, a records management section, or any other function of an organization or community in which the organization and delivery of information is the primary activity. Such activities as the creation and (presumably) later implementation of strategic partnerships within the parent organization, the mentoring that goes on between individuals, participation in team projects (as mentioned in the previous chapter), the aggressive networking of other contacts within the parent organization, and the establishment of essential service relationships between information workers and key management employees in the organization or community are all suitable practices for the furtherance of the cooperative effort in information work.

The term 'strategic partnerships' (or 'strategic alliances', as it is used by some management leaders) describes a phenomenon which has become much talked about in management consulting work during the last few years, but so far its value for the information services field has not been explored. In fact, the concept can be a useful one for those information services executives who are seeking effective cooperative arrangements within the organizations for which their units provide information. A strategic partnership or alliance exists when two or more equal partners resolve that, instead of competing with one another, they will bring their equal expertise to bear on the situation and will work together, as a team, to achieve the goal or goals being sought. In management consulting, such a partnership occurs when one company, which might be the consultant of record, joins with another company to share a project, with each of the companies bringing equal expertise to the work. In the larger business community, as described by Tom Peters, strategic alliances are those companies that compete 'by collaborating in order to avoid competing' (Peters, p. 348).

Such an idea might seem to be an anachronism, particularly in business where the very essence of success is assumed to be based on an exclusive profit-making scheme, but in fact, as Peters quoted an American business leader, Keith Alm, on the subject, the idea of working with a strategic partner significantly increases the opportunities for success:

> Competition by collaboration . . . innovative new partnerships – strategic supplier and customer alliances. . . . We are creating *shared destinies*. And increasingly, the basis for these shared destinies is *shared information. . . . The new currency is knowledge. . . .* Visionary suppliers are beginning to create *knowledge*-based partnerships to share business and *information* with their largest customers. . . . The idea is to . . . create clearly superior customer value that *shuts your competitor out* – preempts him, while creating a *sustainable balance of power* between partners. . . . (Peters, p. 348)

In information services management, those systems that succeed are quite often information services that have evolved from such a partnership, either within the organization or through a combination of efforts beyond (but often including) the organization. While many in the information industry continue to struggle to come to grips with the 'idea' of information as a commodity which can be exchanged, bought, sold and otherwise handled as if it were a tangible asset, there is a long tradition among many of these same information professionals of sharing resources, of cooperating in joint information exchange ventures for the simple reward of providing better information service to their users. Many types of libraries, for example, have long compiled and shared joint holdings lists, so that readers coming into one of these libraries would be able to determine where else an item might be available if it is not physically located at that library. The vast holdings of major university and other research libraries now available through the Internet are a perfect example – and a logical extension – of such an effort. The user no longer needs to go to or even telephone a particular library to determine if it has a title. All he or she needs to do is to call up the various library catalogs via an Internet connection and then, after determining where the material is, begin the process of locating the specific item he or she is looking for.

Within an organization, a similar cooperative effort can pay handsome rewards for information seekers. Consider, for example, a research institute specializing in, say, marine biology. There is a staff of some forty or fifty scientists and associates who do the actual scientific research and a support/administrative staff of perhaps thirty-five or forty people, including an MIS unit, a records management staff, a specialized library or information center, and/or an archives unit for preserving the records of experiments and programs long after the work has been done.

In such a setting, a natural process of organization will have evolved over the years, so that the institute is in actual fact a variety of separate units, each commanding loyalty from its employees and, probably, with little overlapping activity. As organizational incomes rise and fall, as the focus within the research institute changes, sometimes subtly and sometimes overtly, from one area of study to another, these various units will have organized themselves into specific territorial domains. In the efforts of their members to maintain their groups' individual strengths and power within the organization, 'turf wars' will have evolved, and much energy will now be directed to organizational concerns, rather than to the work those units were originally created to perform.

In such an environment, of course, services suffer, and with information services divided between computer services, records management, the library, and an archives section, much duplication of effort takes place and, worse, information customers within the institute frequently find themselves seeking information products and services from the wrong unit of the organization. Clearly a strategic partnership between the information units of the institute is called for, which means that the heads of the various units, meeting as equals, must each agree to use his or her best expertise to think about information services from a 'big picture' point of view. Sometimes the strategic partnership is imposed by senior management, delegating to a senior employee oversight responsibility for information services, and that manager, as the chief information officer, will pull together a strategic partnership or alliance to address information issues. More usual, however, and which would be the likely scenario in the marine biology research institute, efforts toward such an alliance would come from the managers of the departments involved. They would require, at the very least, a commitment to putting aside the territorial concerns that had motivated them as managers in the past.

The motivations for information cooperation within the organization can come about in a variety of ways. Certainly such a pattern might evolve after a specific incident or a series of information 'failures', or, as is becoming more and more common in organizations, there may be some interest, within the organization, for looking to a new way of providing information services for the future. In either case, a cooperative approach will, of course, pay off handsomely for the departments involved, as long as their leaders and their employees are willing to approach the move toward cooperation on an equal basis.

Beyond strategic partnerships and alliances, other cooperative efforts can benefit the information services program within an organization, company or community. Mentoring, for example, has long been accepted both in the management world at large and in the various branches of information services as an appropriate method for bringing people together, usually to advance the careers of the mentees (or protégés, as they are sometimes referred to in the literature). Not much attention has been given to the advantages the mentoring activity brings to the organization, but in terms of information services and the people who provide them, the cultivation and acceptance of a mentoring ambiance within the organization and within the specific information services departments can play an important role in the success of those departments in the delivery of information.

According to Jennifer Cargill, mentoring can be institutionalized by making it 'part of the organizational culture', wherein the pairing of junior staff with established professionals introduces the junior people to the organization and the profession in general (Cargill, p. 13). When the senior information services worker is available to work with the junior employee, he or she makes sure that the employee recognizes the value of cooperation in the various information interactions that will take place. 'A mentor can encourage observation of staff interactions,' Cargill continues, 'and help the protégé to learn from situations by objectively viewing instances as case studies, rather than becoming emotionally involved and losing the ability to resolve problems' (Cargill, p. 13).

Think about, for example, a law firm in which the senior librarian is responsible for working with a committee of the firm's partners to devise a system for organizing the many books, reports and private journal subscriptions that make up the various office collections throughout the firm. While the law library has an excellent system for controlling the materials acquired through the library, many of the lawyers would like to have their office collections similarly organized. Obviously the firm's librarians cannot undertake such a task, but by bringing in one of the junior staff members to work with her on studying the situation, the firm's librarian not only has the advantage of the younger employee's enthusiasm for looking at a project with some room for innovation, but by introducing him to the other members of the committee, his role as a valuable member of the firm's information services staff is recognized. As she and he work together to come up with advice for the various partners, the cooperative arrangement between them as a 'library' team, and between them as a team and the partners' committee, is acknowledged as a beneficial arrangement.

But mentoring, as a mechanism for leading into cooperative arrangements, is really rather passive. What works best in information services is a more direct approach, such as the aggressive networking of other contacts within the organization, that is, contacts with people who are not necessarily information 'customers' or people naturally inclined to be interested in the information function. In the executive offices of a multinational petroleum company, for example, while information interactions between, say, the head of the records management staff and the administrative assistant to the chief public relations officer might be limited, there are nevertheless advantages for them in knowing one another. In order to do his job well, the administrative assistant will, at some point, require guidance about which materials from the public relations office are to be sent to records management and/or to corporate archives. At the same time, in order to have records as complete as possible, the records manager needs to convey to all employees, especially those in administrative positions, the importance of observing established retention schedules and similar requirements for the effective management of corporate records. By aggressively pursuing a working relationship with the administrative assistant (who will more than likely not, of his own accord, be concerned about departmental records), the records manager and her staff will be able to establish a cooperative arrangement that should, if it is carefully thought out, be of benefit to both parties. And in the process, of course, the administrative assistant learns to recognize the role of records management within the company and can connect it to the successful functioning of the public relations department to which he has his primary allegiance.

Similarly, there are employees in every organization whose work requires them to use certain information services, but they do not have a need for – or often an interest in – other information services that are part of the same organization. In the example just given, there may very well be people in the company's executive offices who never think about using the corporate library, even though it has been created and exists for the senior management staff of the company. One manager, for example, has internal staff who provide him with the information he needs, gathered from online database searches, CD-ROM searches, news feeds, and the like, all carried out within the department itself. For this person, occasional meetings with the corporate librarian, or between the corporate librarian and the people in his department who serve as his information providers, can result in better training for those people and a wider range of resources and materials being made available to him. These meetings will, in all likelihood, be initiated by the corporate librarian, but by doing so, she is putting herself forward as an information advisor for this senior manager and his staff, a role which will benefit all concerned.

Such a working arrangement can often lead to one of the most powerful cooperative methods that can be put together, the establishment of an essential service relationship between information workers and key management employees (or a single key employee) in the organization or community. A dramatic example was cited in the popular press a few years ago, when the governor of an industrial state in the northeastern United States took on his staff a 'personal information assistant'. In companies and larger organizations, such an employee would probably be drawn from the corporate library or other information staff and would more than likely continue to be considered an employee of that section, but his or her duties would be primarily related to the work of the individual involved. What this person does, from the point of view of information cooperation, is to bring together the strengths of the information service – regardless of its structure or its position in the organizational hierarchy – and offer them in a 'customized' package for the person or persons being served. As a tactic for effecting advocacy or political sponsorship, of course, such an activity offers incomparable opportunities.

And it is advocacy and political sponsorship which is the subject here. One of the basic concepts about support, of any unit, of any organization, is that it is necessary for that department or unit to have its advocates and political sponsors in order to succeed. Financial support comes to those who demonstrate their value to the organization or community, and while much can be made of the 'innate' or 'natural' value of having an information services unit in an organization (regardless of the 'type' of information services unit it is), the facts of the matter are clear: those who make decisions about the allocation of resources must be made aware of the value of the services those resources support, and establishing a program of cooperation within the organization or community is a respected and time-honored technique for working with these decision makers.

For the information services unit itself, there are benefits from cooperation within the organization, and smart information services executives position themselves to take advantage of every opportunity they have for setting up cooperative activities. In the first place, the information services staff, by working cooperatively with others in the company, know what is going on. They learn which products and services are being worked on, and in doing so, they learn what the organizational focus is at that particular point in time. Especially in large organizations, it is easy for librarians, records managers, archivists, and even computer services staff to be left out of 'the loop', so to speak, and to learn only after certain decisions have been made that they will be part of an implementation program that may require serious changes in the way they do their work in their departments.

Such an example came up after a recent election, when a large public relations firm, one which had not previously been involved with government clients, found itself being invited to bid on a contract to work with a much-criticized government agency. As a decision had been made to improve the public's perceptions about the work of the agency, several 'old guard'-type public relations firms were sought out. The firm in question had a very fine research library, but none of its research staff had worked with government clients before, and as there was little interaction between the chief librarian and senior management in the firm, it was only after the bid had been entered and the contract awarded that the library staff was told of this new 'direction' in the company's work. There was little in the collection pertaining to the subject at hand, and the staff had little experience in this area, so the result was a considerable amount of information outsourcing as the project evolved. Had there been, even informally, a cooperative relationship between the staff at the senior management level and the library staff, efforts could have been made to research the firm's abilities to provide research in this difficult area, and much unnecessary confusion could have been avoided.

As this example demonstrates, a cooperative arrangement between the various units of an organization will enable the information services unit to be able to respond to organizational information needs or, negatively, to fail to do so when there is no such arrangement. Similarly, when there is cooperation between the information services staff and others in the organization, an enhanced role for information services is created. In the situation just described, an established cooperative arrangement would have resulted in the manager of the corporate library being able to go to senior management to describe for those managers the ways in which the library could provide the materials and services needed for the work. Records management people, too, could have researched what work with previous clients might have been related – in one way or another – to the proposed project, thus establishing yet another useful connection. The result of this effort would have been a successful information interaction for senior management and the information services staff, enabling the company to go forward with confidence that the proposal it was submitting would be fully supported by the information staff already in place. As it turned out, additional effort and, worse, additional costs, were required to meet the needs of the company in completing the project.

Cooperation however defined is but one of several routes to effective information provision, but in any movement toward acquiring advocates and political sponsorship for the work of the individual information services unit, the entire concept of cooperation must be considered. No department or section of an organization exists to stand alone, and in today's scaled-down management atmosphere, the information services executive expects his or her staff members to go out of their way to establish cooperative working arrangements with others in the organization or community. The efforts may sometimes seem unusual, or even slightly inappropriate, but if the final result is an understanding throughout the organization (even by people who do not use the information services unit) that information services are vital to the success of the organization, and if the users (both identified and potential) of information services are made aware that their information needs can be met onsite, the efforts are worthwhile.

Eventually, of course, the benefits of cooperation are those which are established by the cooperating parties at the initiation of the effort, but in information services terms, it is important for information executives to understand not only what they and their staffs are bringing to the organization, but to determine what their role is in the larger organizational picture. Libraries, records management units, archives, computer services departments, even consumer information sections all have an obligation to support the overall mission of the parent organization, but part of that support is an understanding of the role of the unit itself and how the information it organizes, manages, disseminates, and sometimes even controls, affects the achievement of that mission.

References

Ashworth, Wilfred. *Special Librarianship*. London: Clive Bingley, 1979.

Burkett, J. 'Library and information services,' in: *Handbook of Special Librarianship and Information Work*, edited by L.J. Anthony. London: Aslib, 1982.

Cargill, Jennifer. 'Developing library leaders: the role of mentorship.' *Library Administration and Management*. Winter, 1989.

Ettinger, Andrew. 'From information to total quality learning: How the information profession needs to change to meet new challenges.' A presentation at the conference on 'The value of information to the intelligent organization', University of Hertfordshire, Hatfield, UK, September 8, 1993. Described in *InfoManage: The International Management Newsletter for the Information Services Executive*. 1 (1), December, 1993.

Peters, Thomas J. *Liberation Management: Necessary Disorganization for the Nanosecond Nineties*. New York: Knopf, 1992.

Waldron, Helen J. 'The business of running a special library.' *Special Libraries*. 62, February, 1971.

Chapter Four

Information vision and information values

The management of information services can be one of the most rewarding jobs in any organization or community, simply because the information
manager has the opportunity to influence the successful achievement of
organizational goals at every level of the enterprise. Whether that person
is the chief information officer in a major multinational corporation, the
manager of a research team in a scientific institute, the chief archivist in a
historical society, the head of a computer services department in a retail
store, or a city or county librarian, this person knows information, knows
how information is used in the enterprise, and is the natural authority for
matters relating to information. Even if that employee is the information
specialist for an organization or community so small that he or she alone is
responsible for information – the classic one-person library, for example
– he or she has a remarkable opportunity to guide others in their understanding of the value of information and information products and services.
No one knows more about information and the information function in
relation to the organization or community than this person knows. She is
– or should be – the point person for information, and everyone she comes
in contact with should know it as well.

Obviously, not all information services managers see themselves in this
role, and for some of these people, the pressures of day-to-day information
provision take precedence over their role as influential members of the
organizational team. Nevertheless, every manager or administrator with
responsibility for information services can play an active role in establishing
and achieving the successful implementation of information policy in
the organization or community, for the benefit of that organization or
community, if he chooses to do so – regardless of the size of the information
services unit for which he has managerial responsibility.

To play this active role, however, requires that the information services
manager matches his own personal vision of information services with
information values already in place or, when necessary, devises the means
for changing information values when, in his own best managerial and

professional judgement, those values are not consistent with the highest levels of information delivery for the organization or community. It is not an easy position to be in, and it can be problematic from time to time, in terms of connecting organizational priorities with departmental priorities (or vice versa), or weighing individual user demands against organizational inhibitions. Despite the difficulties, the payoff, the final rewards in terms of serving organizational information needs with the highest levels of information service, make the effort worthwhile.

For the information services manager seeking to link information vision and information value, the first step is to define her personal information vision, and that personal definition must begin with a look at information services as a whole. Does this person see information services as the delivery of one or other 'type' of information, based on, perhaps, format or location? Or is 'information' anything that anyone needs to know, regardless of where the information is to be found? The answer lies, of course, with one's own definition of 'information services'. As mentioned earlier, the information services concept now includes a broad base of activities which have to do with information, yet each information worker will look at his or her own job as a specific type of work, perhaps not connected with others in the same field.

So the first questions to be asked about one's personal information vision have to do with the role of the information provider. What is it that she is providing? Some, like Elizabeth Orna (as discussed in the introductory pages of this book), would identify information as anything 'that people need to know and apply in their work, to achieve their, and the enterprise's objectives' (Orna, p. 46). Such an all-inclusive definition is becoming more and more accepted nowadays, especially as corporations and other profit-driven organizations need to look at the value of each department. In many such organizations, the move toward integrated information systems is led by the information workers themselves, and senior managers in banks, brokerage houses and other financial institutions are discovering that the best people for organizing such integrated programs are the people who have been managing the firm's information delivery programs all along.

For some information managers attempting to identify their own understanding of information services, a similar definition relates to Orna's, but there is a distinction:

> Information services can most simply be described as a combination of information, technology, and people. . . . A set of activities that provide individuals with relatively easy access to data or information. (Woodsworth and Williams, p. 3)

Certainly for many who work in information services, such a description of the commodity they work with is a useful one. For the purposes of this book, however, information services as a work element can be distinguished even further. While easy access to data or information is part of the picture, *if the information customer prefers to obtain the information himself or herself*, in most cases the question of access is not relevant. For many in information work, it is the information that the user is seeking, not access, and for them it is the responsibility of the information services provider to deliver that information to the user. Access - and questions of ease or difficulty of access - are concerns for the information provider, not the information customer.

Other information workers might take a more limited point of view, thinking of their work as that specifically related to the formats and types of materials collected, and/or types of information sought. Special collections librarians, for example, with their interests in collections organized by format (rare books, say, or phonographic records, or photographic slides) might not see themselves as information services practitioners, for they are primarily responsible for collections of 'things', tangible materials that exist as objects. At the other extreme, however, say at a cosmetics manufacturing company, the information workers who respond to consumer enquiries about their company's products are dealing with information (and nothing else). There are no 'things', no objects attached to their work. Yet both groups of workers are responsible for providing information, and for providing that information when it is sought, and they - and the full panoply of information employees that fall between these extremes - are all information services practitioners.

So there can be a variety of ways in which an information manager can interpret information services, and each manager will bring these personal interpretations to the workplace. This personal vision must be linked, of course, to what each of these people sees as a vision for information services for the community or parent organization in which he is employed, and that is a different matter for interpretation. In this connecting together, as we might call it, the information manager's own value to the organization is of course put on the line, which probably explains why some information services professionals might be wary of putting forth a personal information vision which could conflict with organizational concepts about information. Despite the risks, however, all parties benefit when the information services manager's personal information vision is connected with and influences the overall information picture in the organization.

Consider as an example the executive in charge of the records management operation in a small chemical research company. She knows the importance of quick access to certain records, particularly when an inspection team from the government's regulatory agency is on the premises. For such inspections, staff is not forewarned, and before she was made responsible for records management, she had witnessed the rather frenetic, disorganized and inefficient attempts at compliance that took place whenever such inspections came up. She long ago recognized that the organization of the records management department could be more efficient, and that with the investment of not very much money and a concentrated departmental effort, the records could be reorganized into a more appropriate arrangement. When she was given responsibility for the records section, she put forward her own ideas about the records needed for the compliance inspections and working with the records management staff, she was able to bring about the reorganization.

The hardest part of the exercise, of course, is to step back from one's personal and professional attitudes about information and look at what is expected – in information terms – within the company or organization from a purely objective, purely professional point of view. Conflicts do come up, and the information services manager must make special efforts to determine where his allegiance lies. One company, a manufacturer of electronic components for home entertainment systems, began using a specialist information broker to obtain a new kind of packaging information for developing its packaging products, and the Vice-President for Research, to whom the managers of both the Research and Development Library and the Corporate Information Center reported, was disappointed that it was necessary to obtain information externally. He had advanced to his position through the research arm of the company, he knew the value of information in that work, and he had an idealistic notion that all information used by the company should be generated internally. When informed by his information services managers that the packaging information was not readily available onsite and that engaging the specialized information brokerage firm was the most efficient and cost-effective method for obtaining the information, he was able to recognize the validity of the move to the external commercial supplier.

At the same time, of course, it is important to recognize that there may very well be some level of organizational or community 'vision' about information, and this must be determined. Even if it is not stated in any tangible way, it can be deduced, for it exists even when it is not acknowledged. Certainly for librarians and traditional information providers, this preconception about their work is a major obstacle to newer and more creative ways of doing things. The director of a university library, for example, or the city librarian in any community that takes its library services seriously must constantly balance his or her professional desire to move into innovative and modern information delivery methods with entrenched perceptions among the primary users – academic faculty or local citizens – about what constitutes 'good' library service.

In less public information services organizations, many of these situations arise when a new employee has just come on staff. Particularly when the employee is the manager, and he or she has a vision about a particular way of providing certain information which might be in conflict with established arrangements, conflict can arise as the information services manager attempts to inculcate a 'different' approach to information delivery, the opposite of the electronics manufacturing example used above.

Sometimes, however, such situations come up because the employee has 'grown' with the job, and he is now able to visualize the work from a different perspective than when some of the procedures were first put in place. Consider for example the news library in a small newspaper or a local television station. There are three people on the library staff, and their job is to make sure that the managerial and editorial staff obtain accurate and timely information about the subjects which will be covered in each day's broadcasts or editions. When the library manager first came to work there, he felt that a major effort should be made to clip the large daily papers before the reporters and editors came to work, so he, in his enthusiasm, arranged to arrive at 6.00am in order to have the papers marked for clipping by the time the other two library employees came to work, enabling the editorial staff to have access to the clippings no later than about 9.30 or 10.00. After a few years of this, however, he began to doubt the efficacy of the process, particularly since so much of the industry's data gathering was now electronic and since, from his observations, the clipped materials were used less frequently than when the process had been established. His job then became one of changing work habits for those reporters and editors who used the clippings, for few of them were willing to search the electronic files (even though they were authorized to do so). When he approached senior management with what he thought was a well-prepared proposal for doing away with the clipping service, he met a great deal of resistance and was able to achieve his new electronic clipping service only by carefully observing how other news organizations saved staff time and research resources by utilizing such services. His information vision had changed, and his task now became one of convincing the organization to match its information vision to his, an effort that took considerable manipulation and creative maneuvering on his part.

At this point, organizational culture, the role of loyalty in the organization, cooperative opportunities and similar concerns must be addressed, for understanding these influences within the organization, the information services manager is going to be able to determine information values. In the example given here, the head of the news library eventually had to recognize that the cultural relationship between himself – with his 'new' ideas for information delivery – and the members of the editorial staff was not conducive to an immediate overhaul of the information services process, but by starting slowly, and especially by working with senior management to determine how the workflow of the new library would be more efficient and less labor intensive, he was able to exploit a cooperative arrangement that was already in place, to his department's and the organization's mutual advantage.

There is, of course, always that tension between hard-nosed, businesslike efficiency, with its concerns for the so-called 'bottom-line', and a more generalized and more gentle 'service' approach to the delivery of information. It is here that information vision and organizational values must be matched, for there is nothing worse than attempting to put forward an approach to information delivery which is doomed before it can even be presented. And it is here, of course, that information services professionals have the upper hand, for their history has traditionally been one of service, often to the exclusion of some of the more organizational or departmental activities which are part of their work. Today, information services practitioners recognize that they must balance the two extremes, and managers attempt to put into place mechanisms for helping staff determine how far they can or cannot go in delivering the information. A good example contrasts two large research organizations, one in the private sector and one in the public sector. In both organizations, management attempted to establish regulations and guidelines for the delivery of information products and services, but the different levels of success in the two organizations provides a useful lesson in management balance.

In the public research organization, the success of information delivery was often dependent on which information services employee was assigned to work on the request. Some employees provided a perfunctory search, determined whether or not the product or service could be delivered, and if delivery was possible, appropriate arrangements were made. Other employees, especially middle management employees who also worked as information providers, and who had worked their way up from entry-level positions, often pursued a request for days, determined to provide the information regardless of the amount of time or effort required. The result – for the user group at large – was a spotty record of success with some users being very well satisfied with the service received and others quite disgruntled because so little effort was put into their request.

At the private research organization, on the other hand, queries were subject to a 'one-hour' rule, meaning that if a staff member, after beginning the search, determined that the information product or service could not be provided within one hour, he or she was to go to a supervisor, discuss the query with that person, attempt to 'focus-down' the query through a joint analysis of the query to determine that the search strategy was appropriate. If necessary, the query was turned over to the supervisor, who would contact the original requester, report progress in the search so far, describe the information already located, and determine if in fact the requester realized that the original enquiry would involve considerable additional effort. In many cases, of course, contacting the person requesting the information revealed that what had been obtained was sufficient for his or her needs. In other cases, more work was needed, but having confirmed that with the requester, the supervisor now knew that the effort required was indeed necessary and the request would be returned to the employee – or, more frequently – a group of employees to work on it as a team project, with the search for the information continuing to a successful conclusion.

The difference between the two organizations and their approach to the delivery of information products and services tells much about how an attempt by management to codify and justify individual work efforts can result in a more efficient and effective use of information staff. In the public research organization, the lack of managerial standards (resulting, in this case, in even some of the middle management staff not being able to control the urge to go 'all out' to provide the information) meant that widely varying patterns of service were tolerated within the organization and resulted, ultimately, in costly staff inefficiencies, especially as staff was unable to do routine planning or organizing because they were so busy chasing after difficult information requests. At the private research organization, methods had been devised to staunch the free flow of staff time, so that after certain levels of enquiry, the work was not pursued until a supervisory decision was made to do so.

These examples illustrate two very different approaches to an organizational view of information. For the information services manager who is attempting to determine or identify an organization's information vision, and certainly in seeking to influence that vision, he or she must identify those people in the organization who think – or can be persuaded to think – as he or she does about information. Reference has been made to finding advocates and political sponsors who support the work of the information services unit in the organization. When the information services manager is able to find someone else who believes with him or her in the value of information for the organization or community, justification of information programs and services is made far easier. Sometimes, of course, it is necessary to 'educate' that person about the value of information, but in most cases, such people will have long since identified themselves to the information services manager. They are usually people who are comfortable with information, who have no qualms about working with the information staff in helping them analyze their information requests, and they are frequently very up to date, as lay people, in information matters. Such advocates, as will be seen, can be very useful in helping information services managers connect information vision with information values.

Yet the quest for information values and an information vision (and matching them up within the organization or community) must be directed beyond the information services staff and even beyond the organizational culture. The critical element in the equation is the customer, the information seeker who comes to the information practitioners for specific materials and services. It is this person who must be satisfied, and in the final analysis, until he or she is satisfied, the concerns of the information services staff and senior management are not particularly relevant. If there is any single concept of information vision that must be realized or any single set of information values that must be acknowledged, they are the vision and values of the information customer.

Much is written today about customer service in the information environment, and the subject has become one of major importance in determining the success or failure of information organizations of all types. In today's society (and it does not matter whether we are speaking of 'readers' in a traditional library, 'users' of the various information technologies, or any of the several other descriptive terms that are applied to information customers), identifying the needs and expectations of the customer is now accepted as a guiding principle in successful information services management.

For information services managers, the most important attitude that they can bring to their work is an acceptance of the users' point of view in the information process. Many observers of the information scene have noted that, for the customer, the processes, systems and even the physical structures of information services units are of little or no interest. The customer could not care less about the number of volumes a library has, the physical arrangement of the corporate information center, the storage facilities in which organizational archives are preserved or even the format through which current records are managed. For users, the information services unit has one role, to provide them with the information they need when they need it, and as long as these conditions are met, the information function is successful.

The role of information customers in the establishment of an information vision begins with an analysis of information value to the customer. Within the organization or community with which he or she is affiliated, the customer will have already established patterns of information use, and those patterns reveal particular on-going characteristics that now influence every aspect of information services management. For example, information customers are now very sophisticated about information. While they may not be very skillful at describing what it is they are seeking (and will thus frequently require an equally sophisticated reference interview on the part of the information services practitioner to whom they go for their information), the concept of the information process is very clear in their minds.

That sophistication leads to a second identifying characteristic that customers bring to the information process: they have very high expectations about their information requirements. Of particular interest to the information services manager, the information services and products delivered to these customers must match those needs, as the users have determined what their needs are. In other words, it no longer works for the information practitioner to take an authoritative role, as far as the delivery of information is concerned. The user is well educated and will come to the information practitioner with the full knowledge that his or her understanding of the 'type' of information being sought is what will be provided.

What is happening, as far as the customer's information vision is concerned, is that the information services unit is now providing information to a constituent group of customers who themselves determine the standards of service. This understanding of information management, relatively new in our society, directly affects how information customers think about information and how they perceive the success of the information services and products provided for them.

These concepts all come together in establishing, either overtly or through the efforts of the information services managers, an organizational information policy that reflects the information vision and the information values of the key information players. The policy will include a consideration of an organizational information vision as derived from an understanding of organizational information values, and as filtered through the information services managers in the organization or community. By connecting these information values with the information values of the decision makers and power brokers within the organization, usually through the influence of advocates or political supporters who have access to (and some persuasive authority with) them, information services managers can then do what they do best, that is, bring quality information services into the organization or community for the furtherance of organizational or community goals.

References

Orna, Elizabeth. *Practical Information Policies: How to Manage Information Flow in Organizations*. Aldershot, England: Gower, 1990.

Woodsworth, Anne, and Williams, James F. II. *Managing the Economics of Owning, Leasing and Contracting Out Information Services*. Aldershot, England, and Brookfield, VT: Ashgate, 1993.

Chapter Five

Designing information services

Information services do not exist in a vacuum. They never have and they never will. They are always part of a larger organization or community, and as such cannot be managed without regard to the organization or community of which they are a part. Certainly a computer services department in a business organization, a corporate information center or archives, a records management department in an architectural or engineering firm, or a specialized research library in a scientific institution are quickly recognized as being part of the larger organizational entity and existing to serve the information needs of that organization. Even such supposedly 'free-standing' information organizations as libraries are at some level part of a larger established structure such as a city, county, or other governing authority (for public libraries), an academic or educational administrative authority such as a college or university (for academic libraries) or a school board or district (for school libraries).

There are, of course, those rare occasions when management in an organization (usually a fairly small one) will discover a need for a more formalized structure for handling some of its records, say, or a more economical procedure for keeping track of its reports, files or other materials being referred to by staff members in the course of their work. Even in these situations, however, there is a rudimentary structure in place, even if it is no more than a cabinet with its file drawers full of reports, a wall of cluttered bookcases in each of the offices, or a collection of materials about the early days of the company and how it was organized into the successful functioning unit it is today. When the time comes to delve into these materials and 'get them in shape', when management is beginning to be concerned about the costs – both in labor and in lost opportunities for growth due to an insufficient organization of materials – an information services structure is being formed. Of course it is not called that, and certainly the people involved are not thinking in terms as esoteric as 'information management', but these people, the managers and staff concerned with these issues, are in fact ready to decide upon an organizational structure for their information needs. They are ready to create an information services organization, and with or without the assistance of trained information services professionals, they will come up with something that serves their information storage and retrieval needs. It may be informal or even as disorganized and labor intensive as what went before, but from the point of view of the managers of the parent organization, there is a system in place.

Regardless of how formal or informal the organizational structure of these information services units, certainly none of them, as service organizations, were launched full-grown into existence. Most evolved and were developed to meet specific needs at specific times in the history of each of the parent organizations, and the design of their structure, for the most part, was influenced by and directly in response to particular needs. So to speak about the 'design' of information services is to begin, in most cases, with a 'design' that is already in place. How that pre-existing organizational structure affects the current and potential delivery of information for the parent organization or community is a primary consideration in any analysis of or planning for information services.

Think about, for example, a membership organization for professionals in a literary field, editors, say, of magazines and newspapers. The organization has long maintained a 'library', basically a small collection of literary references, dictionaries, literary handbooks, and, of course, a full collection of the writings and other published works with which the members have been affiliated over the years. Now a new governing board has been installed in the organization, and with the advent of interconnected media, online search capabilities and the like, the board would like to make its 'library' an important literary resource, serving not only its members but offering 'information services' memberships to others who might have an interest in availing themselves of the information facility the board would like to see created.

Several things about the design of information services for this organization have already begun to fall into place. First of all, without the prior existence of a receptive ambiance, the very idea of a major reference center at the organization would not have been considered by the board. So we establish first of all that the ambiance of the place, the institutional culture, is one in which such an activity can take place. Secondly, we look at what already exists. Obviously the services currently being offered, as simple as they are, are of high enough quality that those who use them are satisfied and would, in fact, appreciate a higher level of services. Third, the information services staff itself, the librarians and other researchers who are responsible for providing this literary reference service are open to growth, to seeing their information section move in such a direction that it will be able to provide better and more inclusive services to its constituent user base. Finally, in contemplating any change in the design of an information service, it is important to look at the people who use the service, and it is apparent that in this literary organization, the customers of the service are open to change. The prospects for improved and enhanced information services at the organization look good, and the members of the organization undoubtedly will find themselves the beneficiaries of an exciting and almost state-of-the-art information services delivery program at some point in the future.

Not all information services programs can be so pleasantly anticipated, of course, and a lack of cooperation and enthusiasm in any one of the four components listed above can prevent the accomplishment of a successful move toward new or enhanced services. If the organizational culture is not one which accepts change readily, serious questions must be asked, particularly by the people who will be required not only to initiate the movement toward new or enhanced services, but who will be responsible for their delivery after the change is affected – usually, of course, the information services professionals already on staff. Consider, then, a similar organization to the one described above. This association is also composed of people who are professionals, in this case specialists in one of the more obscure branches of the law, and the organization, like the organization of editors, also has a membership base which supports its services. Among these is an information center which exists to provide members of the organization, the general public and the media with any information they might need about this branch of the profession. Unfortunately, membership in the organization is not a requirement for success in the profession, and the membership numbers are low. Because association income is limited, little support is given to the information center. The culture of the organization, while not exactly 'anti-information', is not supportive, and members of the organization's governing board are constantly questioning the existence of the information center. Like so many specialized libraries in organizations where there is not a supportive culture, the information center is characterized as a drain on the organization's finances. Consequently, the quality of current services is poor, the staff in the information center is unable to respond to any queries with any sort of useful speed, although the accuracy of their response is never questioned. It is just that there are so few staff, and so many enquiries, that the work – much of it having to do with quick turnaround queries for the media – cannot be done to anyone's satisfaction. Needless to say, the staff is overworked and absolutely unenthusiastic about any changes in the work of the department, as they recognized long ago that the association is not willing to provide the resources for supporting a viable information services operation. Finally, of course, in direct contradistinction to the users of the editorial reference library, the few users of the law association's information center invariably go away dissatisfied and do not return with further queries. This drastic and admittedly melodramatic picture provides an example of just how difficult information services design can be, for while the situation here is probably irredeemable, the presence of any one of these negative factors means that the possibilities for designing an enhanced or innovative information services structure for the organization will be extremely limited.

The design of an information services program begins with a look at the information 'problems', at what it is in the organization or community that has brought about an awareness that something needs to be done. In a very real sense, information problems come about because expectations are not being met, and it is the expectations of the information stakeholders, the users, and the decision makers in the organization or community which must be addressed. So a first step is identifying these people, asking about the community or the organization, who the information stakeholders are, what they are seeking from an information services program, and how their information needs can or cannot be met.

How do we describe the information stakeholders? Perhaps some examples can help. While most information services professionals prefer to paint the information user base with a wide brush, the reality of the situation is somewhat different, and there are few information services activities wherein all members of a *potential* user base are in fact participants and recipients of information products and services. The one exception which comes to mind would be the computer services department, for in most organizations where there is such an activity, that is, where the company or organization has made a decision to go to an automated environment, one assumes that all employees or related staff members accept the automated program and put themselves forward for the appropriate training. In reality, the picture is very different, and participation in these activities varies greatly from organization to organization. For example, in one scientific research institute, while the younger (or more 'information enthusiastic', if that can be a descriptive term, for they are not necessarily younger) staff members embrace new technology, others are not interested in learning it and, while paying lip service to its value, limit their own application severely, or direct support staff to take their part. Other staff members, not satisfied with the organization-wide automation environment chosen for the staff, bring in their own equipment for those activities over which they have total control.

In other organizations, of course, the organizational mandate might 'encourage' all employees to participate equally, simply because there may be no other way for them to access the information they need to do their work. The point must be made, however, that while it might be comforting for information services professionals to assume that information stakeholders include everyone who is part of the organizational 'family', there are those for whom information and their interest in information matters varies.

At the same time, however, it must also be recognized that many employees in all organizations recognize the value of information in their work, whether they need to access current internal files and organizational archives, or whether they use the organization's specialized library or information center to access external information which provides them with what they need. In the academic community, as is well known, there are many students, faculty and staff who (despite gloomy reports to the contrary) strongly rely on the information services and products delivered to them by their college and university libraries. And of course in the public sector, there are many people for whom the presence of a local library is a requirement, tied up not only with their concepts of quality of life in the communities in which they live, but frequently with their work as well. These are the people who are the information stakeholders in an organization or a community, and they are the people for whom the design of the information service – whatever its form – will be applied.

But if these are the stakeholders, the *receivers* of the information products and services that will be disseminated from the information services unit, who are the decision makers, the power brokers? Are they the same as the stakeholders, or do they include a separate group of people who, standing apart like some elaborate *deus ex machina*, are in a position to enhance or destroy information services as they are created and as they, the power brokers, see fit? In fact, there are those information services arrangements in which information consumers are incorporated into the 'power structure', as it is so frequently referred to, but in most cases, the two groups are distinct.

In every managerial arrangement, there are those who have power. Whether the distribution of power is formal or informal, there are always those people who, by virtue of their authority, are in a position to make decisions about how organizational or community resources are allocated, about organizational goals and strategies, and, indeed, about priorities of service. These are the people who, in this context, are the organizational power brokers and decision makers. They have the authority to determine how information services are supported within the organization or community, and in that authority lies their power.

In considering the design of an information services program, from a strictly detached and impartial point of view, it is these decision makers who must be looked to. It is these people, the power brokers who have the authority to approve or condemn the very existence of an information services program, whose authority must be addressed. It is their understanding of the value of information which will determine whether or not an information services unit or department is to exist, and if it is to exist, the level at which it is to function. What these people – managers, supervisors, or politicians – expect from an information services unit is the fundamental criteria upon which the structure of the service is established. Ultimately, of course, the success or lack of success of the information services program within the organization or community is dependent upon the success of the service in meeting those criteria.

In many situations, of course, the decision makers in the organization or community are well attuned to the value of information. They understand that quality information services, like other 'basics' of management (accounting, human resources, etc.), are critical organizational components, and recognize that quality information services relate directly to the successful achievement of organizational or community goals. With an emphasis on information management now basic to the training curriculum for managers, the inclusion of quality information services is not the 'foreign' factor of successful management that it has been in years past. For those organizations in which information management is so accepted by senior management, acknowledging and justifying quality information services as part of the basic organizational structure is not the problem it is for some other organizations or enterprises.

For those situations, in which senior management has not yet accepted the validity of information services management as a proper construct in their organizational success, various methods must be applied to raising the awareness of senior management employees about the value of information services. The most useful technique is influence, and it is here that the information services professionals will call in their best advocates and political sponsors. For the information services program to succeed, it will be necessary to enlist the support of people in the organization or the community who are known to appreciate information services, who recognize what information services provide for them in their work (or entertainment, depending on the kind of information services being discussed), and who are accustomed to supporting information services. These people generally can be found among the users of the information service, and in most cases they are people in the organization or community who require information in their work, who already value information, and who are comfortable and easy-going with the information function. They recognize that information services can provide them with the information products and materials more easily than they can obtain them for themselves, and they do not disdain the quest for information as an interference or impediment to the achievement of their goals. They include the obtaining of information as a fundamental activity in their lives, and they can be called upon in support of information services when they are needed.

An honest question might, of course, ask why advocates are needed for an activity as basic as information services, and it is in that point of view that the answer is to be found. Because the quest for information and the products and services that provide information are so fundamental in the lives of most people, the very prevalence of the activity reduces the value of information for many people. Many people assume that since they provide information for themselves, the organization of information is a simple process, not worthy of specialized effort, and they tend to be slightly condescending about information matters. Complicating the situation, of course, are the usual prejudices that many people have acquired about some of the specific types of information services, and they often react, if not negatively, a little contemptuously, to the words 'archives', 'computers', 'library', and so forth. When these people are in positions of authority within an organization or community, they must be persuaded to support information services, and information practitioners, because they as information services practitioners, are naturally suspect. They are, correctly, perceived as having their own 'agendas' about information services, and when this is the case, the influence of an advocate or the intercession of a political supporter can mean the difference between a positive or a negative organizational interaction between senior management and the managers with responsibility for information services.

This is not to say that the specially trained information services professional is not to have a say in the design of information services, or that the design of the program is abdicated to senior management and the advocates. When there is such a professional on staff, or when one is called in as a consultant to management, of course that person is going to play a major role in the design of an information services program. But that person also recognizes that he or she is an *advisor* and *implementor* to management, not the power broker who has the authority to make the decisions about information. Since senior management employees do not have expertise in information management, the best advisors seek (almost instinctively, if they are good at what they do) to learn what it is that the managers want. And when necessary, the use of an advocate as a 'go-between' to influence information policy is a practical step in the realization of information success.

The valuable role that management plays in the design of information services was alluded to in another context, when Ann Lawes discussed the measurement of information quality, in comments that are germane here: 'The establishment of agreed standards of performance,' Lawes stated in an interview, 'is basic to the success of the entire information operation,' and she went on to make a case for fixing standards of service between customers, senior management, and the managers of the specialized library or other information services unit at the outset of the operation (Lawes, p. 4). If such is the case in the establishment of measurement standards, is not the establishment of operational standards equally part of the same process? The design of information services looks to, in fact, *requires* the participation of senior management. For the process to succeed, those involved in the design of information services must find out from management what they want from information services.

The first step in that process, at the risk of patronizing, is to determine what it is that management knows about information. It is often the case in information services that, because we all use information services in one form or another all the time, we assume a knowledge about information delivery and transfer that is not necessarily based on reality. Most of the people we are discussing here, the decision makers in organizations and communities who need information services, are lay people. They are not experts or professionals trained in the study of information, and despite the determined interest that many of these people have in the general subject, they do not have the expertise that information services professionals have. In fact, when it comes to working with these managers and defining information with respect to the organizations for which they have responsibility, information services professionals must guide them in their understanding of the subject. In a study about the development of information systems, Richard Palmer and Harvey Varnet offer a useful definition that connects well with Elizabeth Orna's definition described earlier:

> For the purposes of information management, it is more useful to define information as an intellectual construct that is weightless, indestructible, inexhaustible, and transmittable. It is not used up by use. When materials or energy are used, they are used up. When information is used, there is no diminution of an individual's portion – each person can have all of it. (Palmer and Varnet, pp. 2–3)

Of course most senior management staff recognize that information, however defined, is important for the success of their organizations' endeavors, and that the expeditious flow of information in their organizations is a desirable goal. But in fact many of these people (and many information professionals as well, if the truth were acknowledged), tend to confuse 'information' with the media in which the information is organized, stored, transferred and disseminated, a point well made by Palmer and Varnet:

> Although information is present everywhere, it does not occupy space. As an intangible, intellectual construct, it requires a carrier. Very often information is confused with its carrier. For example, AT&T calls itself an information company, but its primary role is providing the technology for the transmission of information. It is not primarily concerned with what is transmitted. . . . Libraries store a variety of media that carry information, but the media are not information. The 'content' or intellectual constructs carried by the media are information. (Palmer and Varnet, pp. 2–3)

Therefore, the information services professional working with senior management must define for them (and from their point of view) what the information services program will do for the organization or community. The most obvious example, of course, and one that is fast going out of date as the ubiquitousness of automated services becomes a reality in business today, is the question of whether or not to automate this or that service within the organization. If, for example, in a small service company such as a speakers' bureau there is already a computer services department to handle payroll and accounting procedures, the manager of that department might be giving some attention to automating records management. The many diverse records kept on file about each speaker the bureau represents, the various organizations that use the services of the bureau,

the many pieces of correspondence and the contracts retained in connection with each presentation, and similar records occupy much space
and consume much staff time, and the computer services manager, having
organized a workable payroll and accounting system, now wants to turn
her attention to automating the bureau's other records and, wherever
possible, connecting them electronically with the accounting system now
in place.

To bring management into the process, the computer services manager
will take it upon herself not only to approach her manager with the idea,
she will also do some preliminary study of what the current problems are
in records management, with some attention to labor and retrieval costs
for hard copy records. At the same time, from her ordinary knowledge
of the information industry and what is available, and from discussions
with interested parties in the records management department (without
making any commitments, of course), she will form some ideas about the
costs of some of the information management products available, as cost,
even in general terms, is a deciding factor with any management decision,
particularly personnel, training and technology costs. With these very
general terms in mind, she will provide senior management with what it
needs to know in order to decide whether to proceed with looking into an
automated records management program.

A subtext here, or in any movement toward the design of an information
services program, has to do with why senior management personnel
should care about information and how it is organized. If, for example, a
rural community has a small public library available to its citizens for its
entertainment and educational needs and an opportunity exists for the
library to become part of a larger, multi-system consortium, the information
services professionals, the librarians, will need to look very carefully at the
interests of the local power structure (presumably a Board of Trustees
for the library and a supervisory town or county Board of Supervisors or
some other governing authority) to determine whether or not participation
in such a consortium is practical. Despite the obvious advantages to the
librarians, the people who make the decisions must be convinced that
the cooperative effort will bring real benefits to the community. If there are
people on either of the governing boards who believe strongly in their
community's independence, no matter how advantageous membership in
such a consortium will be to the community as a whole, these people are
going to have to be convinced, and they must be convinced on their own
terms. If one of them is active in a local senior citizens organization, for
example, he or she will need to know that membership in the consortium
will enable the local library to provide better services to senior citizens. For
the board member who is an employee of the local government or a local
politician, he or she will need to know that the consortium will provide
contacts with other citizens who have similar responsibilities in other
communities, and that these contacts will provide some level of benefit to

the specific individuals involved. Like the computer services manager in the speakers' bureau, those who are proposing the 'improved' program of information services must do so in terms that relate to the success of the decision makers and power brokers within the organization or the community.

The role of the information services professional in these situations is a vital one, and, in fact, it is a leadership role rather than a deferential one, despite the fact that it is senior management which is being 'led'. All too often, information services personnel see their role as one of 'educating' senior management about the value of information within the organization, but what is called for here is a classic team effort, a situation in which the information services manager works in a peer relationship with senior management in order to bring about a change in the organization that will establish benefits for the organization as a whole. It is, in fact, the concept of the team effort taken to its logical and natural maximum, wherein individual agendas and personal (and professional) territorial claims are subsumed to the common good. The speakers' bureau example, described above, provides an excellent opportunity for three people in the organization to work together successfully to create an improved information services system for the organization, as the senior manager with responsibility for computer services, the computer services manager, and the records manager all work together to a common goal. There is no 'educating' of one or the other about the specifics of the work they are doing, and the relationship is very much one of equals (even though they are not equals in the organizational hierarchy) working together.

For the situation to work, there must be an understanding that the relationship between the people involved is a mutually supportive one. A negative example might be another small business where there is conflict because, although there is an up-and-running automated system for managing internally generated information, senior management in the company continues to resist adding laptops and an external electronic mail system for its sales staff in the field. There is an internal e-mail system, but that does not do a lot of good when the travelling staff must resort to hotel fax machines for gathering the information they need for their work. Despite the best efforts of the computer services manager and the head of the sales staff to negotiate a new arrangement, senior management in the company has established a very hierarchical culture in the organization and all approaches to senior management are, of necessity, deferential. Because there is no peer relationship, as such, between senior management and the other concerned parties, the idea of creating a joint effort to resolve information problems is discouraged before it is even put forth.

In these examples, a new attention to information services has come about because there are information problems that must be addressed. In each case, the motivating question must be: What are we trying to do? At the speakers' bureau, the problem is obvious. There is too much paper, records are difficult to store and cumbersome to retrieve, and since an automated accounting system is already in place, the use of that or a similar system to improve control of the bureau's records will be an improvement and thus an appropriate course for senior management, the computer services manager and the staff member in charge of records management to pursue. The situation at the community library is a little more complicated, since the problem is a 'reverse' problem. While services being offered at the library are good enough, there are better services available through participation in the consortium; the 'problem' becomes one of definition: how does the community – and especially the members of the power structure and the library staff – define 'better'? If the two groups are not in agreement, the 'problem', which for one group may not be a problem at all, is one best left alone, a conclusion with which the other group, the librarians, would not agree, since they see their role as providing the 'best' services they can, as *they* define those services.

The final example is similar to this, in that there is no simple solution to a complicated problem. The 'problem', as seen by the travelling sales staff and the manager of the computer services department in the company, is one that can be readily solved with existing technology. The 'problem' is recalcitrant management, and until some change takes place in the organizational structure of the company, there is not much the sales staff or the computer staff can do about it.

What happens at this point, if there is going to be an attempt to initiate new information services, or enhance existing ones, is that senior management authorizes a study of the existing situation. This study, which attempts to describe the information problems, is then coupled with a needs assessment or information audit. The combination of the two is significant, and the differences between the two complement their validity. Whereas the first is a study of the way things are, the second is a move toward the ideal, a look at the way things *could be*. It is an important distinction, for more than anything else, it represents a move toward an acceptance that information services for the organization or community can be enhanced, and recognizes that the quality of the information services provided for the organization or the community is a critical element in the successful achievement of its corporate mission.

References

Lawes, Ann. 'The information interview: What's expected of an information services executive? In the UK, Ann Lawes has some answers.' *InfoManage: The International Management Newsletter for the Information Services Executive*. Prototype issue, June, 1993.

Palmer, Richard Phillips, and Varnet, Harvey. *How to Manage Information: A Systems Approach*. Phoenix, AZ: Oryx Press, 1990.

Chapter Six
Managing information services

Designing an information services operation points the way. Managing information services, on the other hand, is an altogether different process, and while it would be desirable for all parties in the management of an information services program to have been involved in its design, such an ideal state of affairs is not always possible. But whether or not the information services manager was involved in the design of the program, part of management responsibility includes the ability to match the design of the program to its implementation.

Levels of service

The components of an information services program, its *services* as it were, are based on the needs of the parent organization or community and the people who make up that community. Therefore, as an initial step, information services managers are required to identify, analyze, and coordinate the various needs of their potential user groups (the usual result, in most cases, of the information audit or needs assessment). Part of this process, however, is a determination of the levels of service to be offered, and it is at this point that the realities of the organizational world intrude. Whether they work as records managers, organizational archivists, specialized or public-sector librarians, or in any of the other various fields involved in the provision of information, many information services practitioners see themselves as simply that, as providers of information to all comers, regardless of cost, appropriateness, or any other entity which might limit or otherwise provide a barrier to the provision of that information.

On the other hand, many of these same information services practitioners take upon themselves an authoritative role, a role in which they themselves determine the levels of information services functions to be provided or, indeed, whether they are to be provided at all. This conflict, brought about by a well-intentioned determination to provide universal information services, provides much of the tension in the information services field today. The resolution of this tension can be addressed at the source, so to speak, if the determination of the information products and services to be offered includes not only an objective analysis of what services are needed by the potential users but, equally importantly, what services and products the parent organization or sponsoring community is able to support. Looked at in these terms, the desirable and idealized goal of universal service for all who seek it is quickly mitigated by the realities of what is or is not feasible.

Once the information audit/needs assessment has been completed and the results delivered to senior management and the other decision makers in the parent organization or community, the real work begins. It is now up to the manager of the information services unit to work with those decision makers to establish levels of service for the information services and products to be offered, and to obtain from them a commitment for the resources necessary to provide the agreed-upon services.

A great variety of services can be provided by an information services unit, and any number of authors and commentators have, over the years, identified most of these services. It is now accepted that information services in most organizations and communities can include such activities as the direct provision of information to users (known in libraries, of course, as reference service), the cataloging and classification of information, the creation of filing systems, the maintenance of indexes, subject inventories, current awareness and routing services, abstracts services, the disposal of materials, the training of users (in those organizations which offer self-service information provision), the establishment of policies and procedures, the maintenance of equipment, and archives organization, all of which are directed toward meeting the information needs of the customers, clients and users who come to the information services facility.

Depending on the facility, of course, some services will be emphasized to the exclusion of others, and in a records management unit, for example, such activities as records analysis and the establishment of active records centers will assume a priority role (Wright, p. 302). Public libraries, of course, have a far different focus, stressing the educational and recreational services which they provide but also, as is made clear by any number of authorities (see especially Palmour, as cited in Sager, pp. 97–98), serving as the primary reference center for any number of users in the community. At the other extreme, the information function is primary, and all other work in a specialized library or information center is relegated to a secondary role if it interferes with or provides any barrier to the direct provision of 'information for immediate and utilitarian purposes' (Strable, p. 216).

Given this variety of information activity, it might appear that any attempts to establish levels of service would be inordinately complex. To determine which levels of information service will be provided, to ask what is meant by 'state-of-the-art' in information services could be a daunting proposition, but in fact much work has been done in this area. As far as the collections and services themselves are concerned, accepted guidelines today usually categorize them as being at a minimal, basic, support, or research level. The first three of these (the minimal, basic, and support levels) have for many years been designated by librarians as 'representative', which Talcott (p. 47) characterized as being 'adequate for acquiring a current, basic knowledge of the subject'. On the other hand, 'research-level' collections and services are generally characterized as those materials and services adequate for the needs of graduate practitioners in a particular subject specialty and include, according to Talcott, 'a sufficient number of materials to support research, development, or administrative programs within the subject area'. A final category, those collections and services referred to as 'comprehensive', are those which are accessed in support of ongoing and long-term research development interest in the subject, regardless of the geographical origin of the information.

In addition to looking at the level of materials provided through a library and information services program, it is also helpful to analyze the individual information needs of the customers. Most information needs can be categorized according to the people who are going to be using the information. The following, adapted from Palmer and Varnet (pp. 6–7), might be used to describe most information customers:

1. Information repackagers, for whom information must be totally accurate and who need further information to verify leads they have obtained elsewhere, to check facts, and to determine the value of the information they have chosen (or been asked) to repackage.

2. Problem solvers, for whom information is expected to be precise and quantitative.

3. Decision makers, who need information which must be synthesized.

4. Those who help others, who generally come to an information services unit for directory-type information, using such materials as standards, guidelines, dictionaries, atlases, rules, government regulations, etc.

5. Creative types, who need more expansive information products, including (but not limited to) audio, visual, interactive video, tactile media, etc.

It is also important, in attempting to identify information deliverables for customers, to look at information itself and to distinguish information characteristics which affect its delivery. For most practitioners, the following categories can be useful. For example, levels of service will be affected by the kinds of information being sought, that is, whether it is factual, qualitative, synthesized, 'how-to', or some other type of information; by how frequently it is needed and/or used, that is hourly, daily, weekly, monthly, or annually; by how fast the information is needed, that is, immediately, or later today, tomorrow, later in the week, or within some other timeframe; and of course by how the information is to be used, that is, whether it is for planning, operations, reporting, corresponding, or whether it will be put to some other use or function within the organization or community.

The level of these services will depend entirely on the demands of the unit's customers, on the resources available for providing those services, and on the institutional or corporate culture which supports the information services unit. Think about, for example, the mechanism for providing information for the members of the US Congress. It is about as good as it can be. Turnaround time is minimal, accuracy is so important that special quality review programs are in place, and the necessary resources for ensuring that quality stays high are provided. The reasons are obvious. When asked about support for this very sophisticated system of information management, designed specifically for responding to the information needs of the members and committees of Congress, the chief of the operation has a ready answer: 'Information is power, and we're here to provide information to the people for whom power means a lot' (Jones, pp. 2–3).

Few information organizations are quite so direct in connecting information to their organizational purpose, but no matter what kind of information is provided, service levels relate to that organizational purpose and how it is perceived within the organization as a whole. In the records management department of an architectural or engineering firm, whether information is provided on demand, or whether responses to requests are governed by some regulation built around when they are filed and 'properly' processed, the delivery of those records will reflect the value of the information contained in the records as established by the information customers themselves, and the pressures they are able to bring on both the management of the firm which provides the resources for the management of those records and on the staff of the records management unit which delivers the information.

Levels of service in information management are, in fact, as varied as the organizations and communities in which the information is delivered. While the example of the Congressional Reference Division at the Library of Congress, mentioned above, might seem to be unique, in fact any organization in which information is vital to the successful achievement of the organizational mission is going to require levels of service that cannot be anything less than exceptional. In such information-intensive situations, of course, information services managers are able to demonstrate to senior management specifically how the information services unit impacts upon the success of the organization, and the value of the unit is assured. One of the best examples is at Texas Instruments, described in Helen Manning's 1987 study. Manning reported that at Texas Instruments the return on investment over several years averaged in excess of 400 percent. In one specific year, the corporate investment of $186,000 resulted in $959,000 in quantifiable benefits to the company, a return on investment of 515 percent (Manning, p. [31]). In such an organization, the levels of service are characteristically perceived by all interested parties as high, matching the demands of the customers and the support of senior management.

Resource commitment

It is given that the successful management of any enterprise begins with the accumulation of sufficient resources for the achievement of the goals of the enterprise. In information services management, the delivery of information services and products comes at a price, and while the costs for delivering information can vary as widely as the levels of service offered, there are nevertheless some costs involved. Information services and products are not free, and the effective information services manager expects to spend a certain amount of his or her time communicating with senior management and others in positions of authority about financial matters.

Resource commitment in any organization or community with responsibility for an information services program is based on three organizational components: the value of information services, as perceived by both customers and senior management; the commitment of organizational decision makers to the presence of information services within the organization or community; and an established cost benefit or return on investment realized from the presence of the information services unit or program. However, the usefulness of these components in obtaining support for the information services unit is limited unless the information services manager understands the importance of communicating, to senior management and users alike, his or her own commitment to the information process.

Obtaining a commitment for a policy of ongoing support for information services requires the development of a special relationship between the manager of the information services unit and senior management and the decision makers in the organization or community. Such a relationship can best be established by looking at how management thinks about information services, and several studies have established that there are certain expectations which senior management has regarding information services. These include such expectations as the following, which William S. O'Donnell identified as early as 1976:

1. A clear understanding, by information services personnel, of the role of information services in the organization's operation.

2. A thorough knowledge of the industry or subject specialty of the organization.

3. A detailed knowledge of the organization itself.

4. Forceful insistence on adequate tools.

5. Adequate professional qualifications.

6. Administrative competence.

7. Skill in keeping management informed.

8. A knack for clarifying users' needs.

9. Empathy with users' needs.

10. A sense of participation. (O'Donnell, pp. 179–180)

As this list demonstrates, the information services manager and his or her staff must pay particular attention to the products and services that emanate from the information services unit, regardless of its structure, and carefully avoid moving too far away from the original mission of the unit, especially as it applies to the work of the organization as a whole.

Any number of examples could illustrate this need for keeping the focus on organizational goals, and a negative example comes to mind: In the offices of a small regional news magazine, a company 'information center' had existed for many years, to aid reporters in procuring background information for stories, to provide quick fact checking when reporters and editorial staff needed that service, and to clip and file items of interest from local newspapers, magazines, and any other paper source that the information center's management thought was appropriate. Unfortunately, the clipping process became unwieldy but, worse yet, the center's other services were neglected to the extent that reporters and other editorial staff began to negotiate for themselves to meet their information needs; they learned that they could get along without mediated information services. Over a period of time, as the clippings files bulged and more and more of the center's staff were devoting their time to clipping magazines and newspapers, the established users of the center made less and less use of it, except for the clippings. Needless to say, there were complaints about the service, and when a new information services manager was brought in, an established professional with considerable magazine experience, one of her first actions was to find the funding for an automated online clipping service, available to end users at their desks. Since the reporters and other editorial staff were already obtaining their other information products and services elsewhere (and frequently through automated services), the information center was shown to have outlived its usefulness and was closed down, not because it was no good, but because its primary focus, the clippings service, did not match the information needs of the organization, and as a unique service could be provided more cost effectively through other means.

O'Donnell's list, then, is not an unrealistic approach to information services management. The general tone throughout the list is one which asks of those responsible for information services only that they see themselves as part of the organizational team, and not as separate, stand-alone practitioners who just happen to be working in the organization or community which supports the information services program. This concept can, of course, present the practitioner with a sometimes awkward conundrum, a situation described by Ferguson and Mobley in their book (pp. 4, 6–7) about effective management practices in the specialized library field. Information services professionals often find that they must accept a dual allegiance in their professional lives, one to the company or organization which their information unit supports, and one to the profession of which they are a part. Thus a certified records manager or archivist, a chartered or graduate librarian, or an information scientist will see himself as, yes, a member of the records management, archives, library, or information science profession, but for the effective provision of information services within the community or organization of which his unit is a part, he must also see himself as an employee of that organization. In fact, for most practitioners, the situation is not one of a 'dual' allegiance at all but of two allegiances in which one, the allegiance to the company or organization, must take precedence over allegiance to the profession. It is a situation which, for some practitioners, causes stress, but even for them, only until they think about which of these allegiances is responsible for providing them with their salaries, after which the idea of a dual allegiance ceases to be a stressful one indeed.

This division, sometimes formal and at other times simply a vague and intangible tension, affects the provision of information services in most organizations and communities and must be recognized and acted upon. Surely O'Donnell's list is not exhaustive or necessarily complete, yet these management expectations, the ones he lists and many others, are not always matched with the expectations that information services managers have about their own work. This state of affairs was clearly demonstrated in an important study done by James M. Matarazzo, Laurence Prusak, and Michael R. Gauthier in 1990. Surveying the immediate supervisors of corporate librarians, the study produced interesting and rather unexpected results about how these people felt about the information services units for which they were responsible, and although the respondents were not themselves information providers, the fact that the information providers reported to them added a different dimension to the usual perceptions information services professionals, especially librarians, have about themselves and their work. And although the study was concerned with corporate libraries, an objective reading of the authors' conclusions suggests that many if not all of these conclusions are applicable in the other branches of information services. The brief conclusions of the study are worth quoting in their entirety:

- Librarians evaluate their performance based on standardized library methodologies. Their managers use far different, and often subjective, evaluation criteria.

- There is little managerial consensus on how the library adds specific value to the firm's performance or how value should be measured.

- Librarians have little say in the firm's information policies and mission. Few respondents could state what exact function the library performs within the firm's information structure.

- Growing end-user usage of database systems and other information technologies will have a serious impact on business operations as well as on the role of the library within the firm. Will the librarian perform as purchasing agent, gatekeeper, network manager, internal trainer, information specialist, or chief information officer? Librarians and their managers have done very little planning on this critical issue.

- There is still a strong reservoir of goodwill and affection for the library and librarian – often based on an intuitive 'feel' that the service is valuable and worthy of continued support. However, in the increasingly volatile business climate, it is questionable whether libraries can grow based on these forms of approval. . . . (Matarazzo, Prusak and Gauthier, p. 1)

The message that comes through from these conclusions is clear. Information services managers must re-direct much of their thinking about organizational support for the services that their units provide, and they must do so in ways that establish that they are active participants in the overall quest for success in the achievement of organizational or community goals. They must assume an information 'vision' for the organization or community, and they must use their persuasive and entrepreneurial skills to get others – particularly the power brokers in the organization or community – to buy into that vision, so that when they have established an information policy, they, as information specialists, will be full participants in the process that establishes, implements and reviews information policy.

In the evaluation of information services, those who manage information services units must link their evaluation methods to those of the company or the community as a whole. Which means, of course, that if they are records managers, they stop talking about the number of items filed or the number of subjects created and concentrate on what the provision of requested records did for the customers who requested them. Similarly, MIS employees must stop talking about the technical and admittedly 'glamorous' hardware and software, telecommunications systems, and other products related to the information technology they manage, and instead concentrate, for the benefit of senior management and customers alike, on how these systems save time and money or otherwise financially benefit the organization.

In fact, Judy Labovitz, a corporate librarian, takes these concepts even further, and advises information services practitioners to assume more specific responsibility in the resource-allocation process. Speaking to a group of corporate librarians, Labovitz urged them to see themselves more as entrepreneurs engaged in selling their information services and products to upper management:

> No matter how efficient you are, or how satisfied your users are, you still have to sell the library to those who control the purse strings. Here is where I feel too many librarians fall short. I strongly believe the library world would fare a lot better if more librarians looked at themselves as entrepreneurs. After all, we are a small business competing in the marketplace for a share of the pie.
>
> My situation is no different from yours. I must fight for money, space, and people. To do this I must sell the value of the library to upper management so that they will be willing to pay for library services. If I don't do this well, then I get less of the pie. Notice I have not blamed upper management for not understanding the intrinsic value of the library. If I get less of the pie, then I have failed to communicate to management in a language they understand, and that is my problem, not theirs. (Labovitz, p. 9)

Think about, for example, the information services operation in a large manufacturing company, a producer of household appliances, say. Such an organization will have any number of departments or sections concerned with information, from the provision of research data to the collection, maintenance, and dissemination of internal administrative and/or compliance records. When the management in any one of these units must approach senior management about support, certain concepts are invoked and certain terms are always used. 'Customer satisfaction', 'process improvement', and the like are explicitly referred to, and inevitably the information services managers offer senior management quantifiable data to support their statements about these concepts. These terms, and others like them, are the language of management, and the information services managers long ago learned that their most important communications skill is the avoidance of departmental (or professional) jargon and the inclusion of managerial terms, just as Labovitz proposes.

There are, nevertheless, sad and negative examples as well. A major insurance company, with several libraries at its corporate headquarters, decided to close its corporate library. Other libraries at the same site, such as the law, marketing and engineering libraries, were not closed. The company was roundly castigated by librarians, vendors, and other corporate information workers, and much attention was given to the event in the professional media, with most of the 'blame' for the company's actions falling on a new senior manager who decided that the company was not getting enough return on its investment. Despite the emotional responses from the affected workers, the decision was not a capricious one, as senior management had looked at overall corporate operations and had brought in a specialist consulting firm to study information flow within the company. When the conclusions of the study pointed out that the corporate library was not used enough to justify its costs, and when it was made clear that primary information use was individual, provided to staff through a sophisticated automation system which was accessed at their desks, the company had no choice but to close the library. By that time, of course, it was far too late to save the jobs of the library staff. If, however, the corporate library's managers had, in fact, re-focused the department's efforts to providing different services (including training, consultations and information 'navigating' for end users as they attempted to get up to speed with the company's automated information system), their services would not have been done away with. The staff would have continued to offer services, but they would have been different services. The bottom line was not difficult to find: the services of the corporate library, as structured by the current library managers, were not needed within the organization.

Fortunately, the example given here is, in fact, atypical. In most organizations, when there are problems in communication between senior management and those responsible for information services, what we are looking at, in most cases, is indifference. According to Herbert S. White, indifference about information services is the 'greatest problem' information services managers have in working with senior management. The decision makers in the organization who control and allocate resources do not necessarily *oppose* the presence of an information services unit in the organization, nor do they have any particular concerns or perceptions about the value of the services being provided. They are, in fact, merely indifferent, and information services managers must establish routines and procedures for serving these people as well as their 'usual' constituencies in the organization or community. According to White, doing so:

> . . . Requires an understanding of who these people are, an attempt to orient both collection and services to their usually specialized needs, and a conscious plan to win over a group of people who are not instinctive or experienced users. The dictum that individuals will support those services which they find personally useful holds for management as well, and management has the power to downgrade or eliminate services they do not use in order to provide greater support for those they do. (White, p. 104)

Eliminating indifference is a major step on the road to resource commitment, and with such support comes the opportunity to seek those further resources which are required for enhancing and improving even those information services and products that are already successfully offered for the organization or community. Such happy results are a benefit of what Charles Bauer has characterized as 'managing management', that is, positioning oneself and one's department or operation so that the value of the services provided is not only supported, but supported to such an extent that it brings clear, tangible results in the movement toward the successful achievement of even idealized or at least workably positive goals:

> Managing management is an earned privilege. It means continuous, arduous work, effective planning, proper supervision, productivity, coordination of efforts, salesmanship, and reputation for having good sense and a reliably concerned professional attitude. To become a part of management, however, take the initiative and learn how to work with management. What is earned in that role is top management's acknowledgement. Once that is attained, it is not too hard for a manager to ask top management for special needs and even some favors. (Bauer, p. 216)

Managing information services

Understanding the connection between established levels of service in the provision of information products and services within an organization or community and the role of resource commitment in the process, it is appropriate to move into a discussion of management principles as they are applied in the information services sphere. While there are certainly any number of definitions of management and descriptions of the management process, when discussing information services management, such definitions and descriptions must be put into an 'information' context.

To begin with a textbook approach, Andrew D. Szilagyi, Jr., whose *Management and Performance* serves as a starting point for many management students, defines management as 'the process of integrating resources and tasks toward the achievement of stated organizational goals' (Szilagyi, p. 5). Most information services professionals would have no argument with this statement, and in fact would find it relatively simple to connect these general terms to what they do, coming up with something along the lines of 'the process of combining *organizational* resources with *information* resources and integrating these resources with *information-related* tasks to provide the information – in all its forms, and internal as well as external – that enables the organization to achieve its stated goals'. The key, of course, is in the statement of the goals, the mission statements of both the information services operation and the parent organization or community as well, and in the agreement between senior management and the managers of the information services unit about performance measures, levels of service, and the allocation of resources in the achievement of the goals required for the implementation of these mission statements.

In the information services field, most discussions of management principles avoid defining the term itself and rely instead on describing what managers do or what their managerial responsibilities are. Ellis Mount, for example, has long been established as one of the foremost academic authorities in the management of specialized libraries and information centers, and his list of management responsibilities serves well as a guide for what is expected of management personnel in information services. There are, according to Mount, eight primary responsibilities for the information services manager:

1. Relating to top management.

2. Planning.

3. Budgeting.

4. Organizing and staffing.

5. Supervising.

6. Marketing.

7. Evaluating operations.

8. Using management tools. (Mount, pp. 30–31)

Helen Waldron, on the other hand, looked at the manager's responsibilities (she called them 'objectives') and connected the work of the corporate librarian with the overall corporate information and operational picture:

> The first objective, then, will be to get a clear picture of the company's struc- ture so that the librarian and the library can identify with its main objectives; and second, to acquire a thorough understanding of company policies within which the library will be operating - the quickest way to perdition is to attempt to operate in conflict with those general policies. The third objective will be to begin the establishment of harmonious relations - with users, with peers in the organization, and with management strata above and below. (Waldron, p. 65)

It is generally accepted that successful management combines four func- tions. Although given different names by different people, Szilagyi has identified these functions as planning, organizing, leading, and control (Szilagyi, p. 68), and most management authorities use these terms or terms very similar to them. Understanding these four concepts, and how they are applied in an information services management context, ensures success for the information operation in any organization or community. Planning, for example, is the process by which information services managers establish a framework in which information activities are performed, with the happy result that the information services unit is offering the services that its customers need (or, conversely, failing to offer needed services and becoming, in the process, a liability rather than an asset to the organization or community for which the information services unit is to provide infor- mation.) Organizing the work, that is, establishing order and function to the design of the information services unit, enables information services managers to devise work patterns and relationships which result in the successful delivery of information products and services. Leading has primarily to do with direction, but not, as is so often assumed, with auto-cratic behavior. The true leader in an information environment brings leadership skills which encourage staff to respond to information requests not because they *must*, but because they want to, for the benefit of all concerned. Control and accountability are those elements of information services management that ensure that the work gets done, that the workers are productive, and that the information customers are satisfied with the responses they have to their enquiries. Finally, although not specifically designated as one of Szilagyi's primary management functions, change management and adaptability relate to each of them separately and to all of them together, as these functions affect the delivery of information products and services. As a point of focus in the modern information environment, in a society in which the very elements of society have become change oriented (and nowhere more so than in information services), the acceptance of change and the skillful management of change within the workplace have valuable implications for information managers.

Planning for information services management

The framework in which information services are performed, the structure of the information services unit, so to speak, is the result of an ongoing planning process. It begins with an assessment of the environment of the organization or community, and requires that management in the informa-tion services unit take an objective look at the context of the operation. Why is the unit there, and what services is it expected to provide? Are the services, in fact, relevant to the work of the organization, and if so, what specific kinds of work (or departments within the organization or community) are supported by the information provided by the unit? Some years ago, the staff library at a large veterans' hospital was faced with closure, and library managers had no problem discerning why senior management had targeted the unit. It was not used as much as it should have been, and much of the in-depth 'scientific'-type research was carried on at nearby academic or research institutions, with which many of the staff were also affiliated. In assessing the environment in which the library was operating, the managers of the library realized that there were other needs at the hospital which they and their staff, as organizers of information, could meet. Much planning and re-organization went into the process, but eventually the hospital library merged with the patient records section, in order to provide not only superior back-up information which could be specifically related to individual patient care, but also to re-organize and make more efficient the management of patient records within the hospital. The first step in the planning process – assessing the community and organizational environment – provided library management with the information and the inspiration to move into a wholly new, but especially effective, information provision role.

Other steps in the planning process, of course, are not quite so spectacular. For example, evaluating current services and resources may sound like a routine process, but when the questions of the information audit or needs assessment are asked, suddenly many new agendas, relating to various people within the organization who have become accustomed to the systems in place, come to the fore. The questions asked, however, must be asked, and it is necessary for information services managers to objectively analyze the answers to such questions as:

- What information services and products are on offer from the unit?

- Are they adequate, or is something missing?

- Do information customers go elsewhere when they should be coming to this information unit for products and services? If so, why?

- What is the resource picture? How is the unit funded?

- Are there problems? Is anyone complaining about services? Which ones? Why?

One of the beauties of the planning process is that it allows information services managers to think in terms of how good the products and services of the operation could be, yet one of the more disappointing aspects of the process is that such goals must, in many cases, be postponed until present needs are met. Using the results of the information audit, managers can determine the specific role or roles of the information services unit in the parent organization or community, but the specific question which must be answered, and which is hard for most planners, is the one that asks what kind of information services operation the organization should have at the present time. Instead of dealing with the future and an ideal scenario, the information services manager must cold-heartedly determine what services and products are needed to meet present needs, as the information services unit's customers perceive those needs. The managers can direct, suggest, and cajole, but in the final analysis, at this stage of the planning process, specific current needs are the ones which must be addressed.

At this stage, however, it is time for developing goals, objectives and priorities for the information services unit, and for developing the specific and immediate strategies for achieving those goals. Think, for example, about a scientific organization, one which sends archaeologists into the field and which has a fully integrated information services program at the organization's headquarters. Internal and external information is readily available through personal computers at individual workstations, and at first glance, the information system would seem to be state-of-the-art.

The only flaw is that, because of funding restrictions, no system has been developed for the scientists in the field to communicate with the main office, and without portable or laptop computers and satellite connections, the archaeologists' findings continue to be sent in manually. Until changes can be made in the funding of projects, information services management is hampered and progress is stalled.

Continued monitoring and evaluation, however, is the next step in the planning stage, and as the example demonstrates, with appropriate record keeping and documentation, it will soon become apparent that changes are necessary, and senior management will incorporate those changes.

There are, of course, certain factors to keep in mind in planning for information services management, and the most obvious which come to mind have to do with such things as changes in a constituent user base, new service demands and, connected with them, the new demands created through new technological developments. CD-ROM technology is the best example of this phenomenon, for it was not so long ago that writers and editors at a cultural magazine, say, would be reluctant to ask research staff to search online, simply because the costs of online searching (especially if the costs were charged back to individual departments) would make them think twice before asking for information. As younger members of staff enter the workforce, however, they have become accustomed to using the latest information products, usually through their graduate training programs in journalism or communications, and they are not at all reluctant to do their own searching, often preferring CD-ROM products simply because such usage does not incur online charges. In fact, in some such organizations it is the younger writers and the junior editorial staff who will request the newer technology, leading the information services staff to new and better ways of providing the information they, as the information customers, need.

Strategic planning

Once called, euphemistically, 'long-range' planning, strategic planning has come to mean something quite different. The 'long-range' aspects of the process long ago took flight, simply because, during the last couple of decades, changes in information services management (and in society at large) became so drastic and so frequent that planning for anything beyond four or five years became an exercise in futility.

In information services, strategic planning has been defined variously, and a number of good texts and guidelines are available for information services managers who wish to engage in this useful activity. The primary difference between planning, as a management tool, and strategic planning is that the latter can be especially effective in preparing an organization or community and its constituent parts, including an information services unit, for the future. As Ferriero and Wilding have pointed out, strategic planning assumes that change is both desirable and inevitable. Strategic planning also assumes 'that organizations exist in a dynamic relationship with their environments, and that for an organization to thrive, it must be in a constant state of change in order to maintain a high degree of relevance' (Ferriero and Wilding, p. 3). In accepting this premise, information services managers recognize that much of their work is customer driven, and that they themselves, while performing as proactively as they can within the environment in which they work, must at the same time react to customers needs, as those needs change.

Strategic planning has a number of goals, all of them concerned with what the organization and/or its constituent units will be required to offer in the future. Inherently, according to one authority, a strategic plan will accomplish a number of significant goals:

- It will bring the purpose of the information services unit into focus, by concentrating on the unit's mission.

- It will set forth what the information services unit is to accomplish, its goals.

- It will show how the information services unit will accomplish its goals, that is, it will identify strategies.

- It will optimize the match between strategies and resources, including human, physical, financial, and time resources.

- It will require senior management and other key personnel within the organization to work together and with information services management, for the benefit of the organization or community as a whole. (Asantewa, p. 1)

In terms of its benefit to the organization and the information services operation within the organization, the strategic plan looks at a broad spectrum for the future. It begins with the environmental 'scan', as it has come to be known, an extremely useful device which provides not only an analysis of the values that impact upon the information services operation within the organization or community, but a reference point for envisioning what the information services operation can be - and do - at some point in the future. This scan can look at the organization as a whole, and the role of information services within the organization (as Newsome and McInernery have done), or it can concentrate specifically on the environment in which the information services operation functions, which is the approach Ferriero and Wilding take. They define the environmental scan as 'the systematic review and analysis of data' about the universe in which the information services unit operates, a review which, inevitably, provides much useful information about the information services unit and what it can contribute to the organization or community.

A strategic plan is presented intentionally in idealized, 'best-case-scenario' terms, to stimulate creative thinking and to enable all participants to look as optimistically as they can at the services under review. In fact, what the plan determines, in terms of information services, is what information products and services might be made available over a period of time, relating to opportunities within the environment in which it operates; what the unit is able to do, in terms of present and future resources; what senior management (of both the organization and the information services operation) want it to do; and, in terms of ethical and societal issues, what the information services unit should be doing for the organization and the community of which it is a part.

Organizing information services

Organizational and sub-organizational functioning determine the structure of the information services operation, and the achievement of organizational goals remains paramount and a constant motif throughout all efforts to organize information services. Five factors contribute.

Positioning

The role of the information function within the parent organization or community combines with the perceived value of information in organizational, effectiveness, and societal terms to determine how the information services unit is to be positioned within the organizational structure. In a high-tech scientific or research company, in which the company's profits depend on continuous access – at each employee's desk – to the most current, accurate information, each section of the company which provides information, or affects the delivery of information, will be positioned as an important part of the organizational structure. And, as indicated in the earlier quotation from Herbert S. White, the more important the delivery of information is to the decision makers and senior management in the organization, the more prominent the information function becomes in the organization.

On the other hand, a community sends a very clear signal about the position of its public library when funding is reduced and library services are available for only a few hours each afternoon in order to accommodate school children doing their assignments. Information services, except for those provided for the schoolchildren, have very little value in the community, and the effectiveness of the library is so limited that the position of the library could not be much worse.

Of course the position of the information services unit affects its organization. Senior management will provide funding, staff, and organizational support for those services it values, and such support obviously enables the information unit to function as a 'Class A', 'Class B', or 'Class Z' type of operation. The best examples are found in the financial community. Visit any top-of-the-line financial services company, enquire about the level of information provision, and you will be shown into a corporate library, research department, or information center that leaves you stunned with admiration. The information function is centrally located, its staff well paid, well dressed, and the very embodiment of quiet authority in the delivery of information, and the ambiance and facilities are designed to provide the utmost confidence in the information provided. In most such companies, the information services manager, as an essential executive in the company, sits on senior management committees and is recognized, quite intentionally, as an active participant in the management of the company as a whole. In this organization, senior management has long ago recognized that the highest quality of information management is critical for the financial success of the company, and the information unit and the services it offers reflect that recognition.

On the other hand, a stroll into the library of a private alumni club in midtown Manhattan provides the visitor with a rude awakening. Despite the fact that the club is connected to a university and would be expected to provide services recognizing the 'intellectual' side of is members' interests, the library at the club is a mess. The rooms where the books are housed are far away from the usual traffic flow within the clubhouse, and while attempts have been made to provide a 'pretty' ambiance ('like a library in one's home', the club's general manager remarks), the resulting efforts have not created a serious library environment. Library staff consists of two or three misfits who would not be able to hold down jobs elsewhere, visitors to the library are discouraged from coming into the library rooms, and the ambiance is one of difficult – if not impossible – access to information and information products. Members of the club dislike using the library and in the organizational structure, the library is somewhat akin to the housekeeping department or the front door staff. While little money is invested in the operation of the library, much is spent on other functions at the club, and such departments as those related to the squash courts, the swimming pool, and the food service operation consume enormous resources, of which the club's management committee approves wholeheartedly. The position of the library – in this case – not only affects the organization and services of the library, it essentially *determines* how the library is organized and what services it will (or will not) provide to its constituent users. The library is relegated, sadly, to a non-essential, relative minor role in the overall club operation.

Levels of service

Already alluded to in a different context, the levels of information services offered for the parent organization or community will determine, to a large extent, how the information services unit is organized. If the information unit exists to provide simple, fact-checking types of information without any proactive or other special initiative from the unit's staff, a simple organizational structure is all that is called for. Depending on the amount of information to be provided, the staff can range from one person, whose responsibility includes all aspects of the information process from the initial reference interview with the client to the final disposition of the enquiry through the delivery of the information products and services sought by the client. At the other end of the spectrum, a parent organization or community might seek not only the information itself from the information services operation, but guidance and direction in the building of the information infrastructure within the organization or community. In this case, the organization of the information services unit will require a more sophisticated approach, usually with interacting layers of responsibility with other departments and sections in the parent entity of which the information services operation is a part.

Examples can be found in the research departments of certain magazines which are published regularly. On the one hand, a small, special-interest magazine with limited sales and a small readership will not usually require a complicated research operation. Fact-checking, totally reactive by definition, will be assigned to this or that member of the magazine's staff, and information provided will usually be requested by editorial personnel who have already completed what might be referred to as 'basic' information about the subject at hand. In a larger magazine, not only will there be an editorial library, a corporate research center (if the magazine is part of a larger corporate entity), and a separate research staff, but all of these information units will be expected to initiate and provide sophisticated information services in anticipation of customer needs. For example, in editorial meetings, as subjects for stories for the magazine are discussed, the director of one or more of the information units will participate, in order to provide editorial personnel with guidance about how much research can be provided in-house, how much will require external information, and similar 'judgement calls'. Additionally, once the subject for a story has been accepted and assigned, information staff will begin research activities in that subject area so that editorial staff will have sufficient background information to proceed with the assignment.

A final consideration relating to levels of service concerns the actual delivery of information, specifically the role of the end users. Is the information services staff to provide the information, or is it in place to navigate the end users to the appropriate sources for their own searching? As the growth of automated information services proceeds, many users are finding that they come to the information services staff as a sort of 'last resort' after they have found for themselves the initial information they needed. When they want more, they turn to the more experienced staff of the organization's information unit for guidance, and the extent of this activity, particularly as it relates to training and similar labor-intensive functions, plays a large role in determining the organizational structure of the information services operation.

The constituent user base

Simply put, the information services unit exists to provide the information that the customers require for their needs, and the organization of the unit must reflect basic customer service precepts. These are usually summed up in such phrases as, 'How easy are you to do business with, from the customer's point of view?' or, similarly, 'Quality of service, as perceived by the customer, [is] the number one driving force for the operation of the business' (Harps, p. 1, and Albrecht, p. 20). For the information services executive, adherence to these customer services principles becomes a critical benchmark for successful information provision, and attention to customer service is built into the operation.

Picture a trucking firm where a staff of twelve people collects, files and retrieves the hard-copy receipts of each of the transactions the firm engages in. As the truckers complete their jobs, the documents are turned over to a central records unit, which organizes and files them according to a set procedure. A new automated scanning system has now been installed and is expected to be up and running within a few weeks' time, and the expectation is that fully eighty percent of the records management staff will be reassigned, since the new system will replace much of the manual labor involved in handling these documents.

After an initial period of concern, the records management staff is now enthusiastic about the new system and is anxious to begin using it, not only because it will free over half of them to move on to other, more interesting work (already determined by management, and with staff's agreement), but also because the 'reduced' records management staff will assume greater authority and control in the handling of these important documents, which are a critical link in the company's own customer service structure. Whereas in the past when one of the firm's customers had a question about a bill, because of the time lag in searching for, retrieving and delivering the document, the transaction took no less than a week or ten days (with the resulting customer complaints), the new system is designed to provide instant access for the operators and service representatives who deal with the customers.

The snag in the operation is the firm's automated services department, whose manager, in reluctantly agreeing to acquire and install the scanning system, was forced to postpone, at least for a while, her primary goal, of automating the company's personnel records. Now that the scanning system is in place, she and her team have returned to their main interest and are working diligently with the Human Resources Department in analyzing the company's requirements as far as automated record keeping is concerned for that function. Unfortunately, only her staff is qualified to train the records management people in the use of the new scanning system, since they negotiated the deal and supervised the installation. When vendor training was suggested, she had refused it, in an attempt to keep the cost of the scanning system as low as possible, so the records management people cannot turn to the vendor for training. At the same time, when any of them approach the automated services staff, they are always put on 'hold' or told the call will be returned, which it is not. The records management staff, the 'customers' of the automated services department, are in fact in a sort of 'limbo', anxious to begin using the new system and prevented from doing so because the people – in their own company – who have the information cannot or will not provide it. The situation is, of course, one of much tension and strained relations, and eventually senior management will be brought in to arbitrate and all parties will become resentful and anxious. By ignoring a basic customer service principle, that you follow up with your customers (or at least provide the opportunity for them to be trained in using whatever it is that you have provided for them), the automated services department has effectively halted the implementation of what was intended to be a very useful and beneficial new system.

Resource allocation

How an information service is funded, and how well it is funded, contributes directly to its organizational structure. Often assumed to be connected with staff size, simply because innovative and creative information delivery systems require staff time for conceptualization prior to creation, the allocation of resources in fact has more to do with management concepts about what role information is to play in the parent organization or community. All too often, senior managers assume a knowledge of information services which is based, unfortunately, on preconceptions that, in present circumstances, have little to do with reality.

A misperception common in the last decade, but fortunately not so common nowadays as managers become more educated about information services, is the old idea that automating a service will enable management to reduce staff. In fact, the body count often stays the same after an automation system is introduced, and in many operations simply grows as staff, freed from the drudgery of routine manual clerical work, can devote its attention to more innovative and better service operations. The acceptance of new ways of doing things simply means that the present staff can do what it has to do better than it did before, and that often results in a higher level of service than had been originally delivered.

It falls on information services managers to ensure that the decision makers in the organization or community understand the value of the information provided and the return on investment in the resources allocated to the information services operation. To do this, the information executive must make every effort to educate senior management in the three areas that Betty J. Turock has identified:

> The economics of information services will never be understood thoroughly without incorporating facts about users, their uses of information, and the effects of that use. (Turock, p. 103)

As part of the information unit's customer service plan, a thorough review of all constituent users, the various units and organizations they represent, and any potential users not currently served must be initiated. The process is not an easy one, but it is required if senior management is to recognize the return on investment in information services, and at the risk of over-stating the case, emphasis must be placed on the third of Turock's criteria, the effectiveness of their information use.

A useful contrast can be seen in the attempted closure of two corporate libraries, described in a newsletter for information executives. The story is worth repeating:

> In today's competitive environment, even in the provision of information services, there is no such thing as a self-evidently 'good' operation or depart-ment. If a corporation decides to do away with its corporate library or informa-tion center, financial reasons are usually cited. Management decides to do away with or restructure departments for one of two reasons. Either the department no longer provides the services it was originally created to provide, or those services can be obtained more cost effectively and more efficiently elsewhere.
>
> In one recent corporate library closure, the trouble began with a corporate reorganization. Nine months before the library was closed, the library was repositioned to report to a different manager. This senior employee was concerned that although the library theoretically served the entire corporation, its primary funding came from one specific department.
>
> Using the assistance of an external consulting firm, the new manager was able to establish that not only was the corporate library costing the one depart-ment large amounts of money, its services were generally unknown throughout the company and only a small group of 'core users' were accessing its services with any regularity. Unfortunately, the studies that made this point were not conducted with the cooperation or through the facilities of the corporate library, and although the manager of the library was aware that the work was being done, she was not 'invited' to participate in the evaluation process of the studies that determined how the core users could have their information needs met more effectively using other information resource agencies and providers.
>
> When the studies were finished, the corporate library was shut down, without fanfare and without much concern being expressed throughout the organization.
>
> Across town, the manager of a research library in a utilities company began to hear rumors that there would be a corporate reorganization, and that the research library was being looked at as a candidate for closure. Having a good

relationship with her senior managers, the manager of the research library brought the subject up. She was reassured that the research library was in no danger, that its services were valued, and that in any reorganization, she would be notified before the closing of the research library was seriously considered.

Not being a naive person, the library manager decided to take matters into her own hands. She felt that perhaps some preventive steps were called for, so she organized a meeting of her staff and, with everyone agreeing to partici- pate, began to ask selected engineers in the company, known to be users of the research library, about the services they received. The questionnaires were short, to the point, and required little of the targeted engineers except a few minutes of their time.

What was remarkable about the responses was the awareness-raising among the users. Many of them replied that they had never even thought about the research library, one way or another. It was 'just there'. Now that they were being asked to evaluate the services received, and particularly to determine how the library aided them in their work, they suddenly found that they had a valuable asset at hand, and they (like converts everywhere) began to talk among themselves and with other company employees about the library and how important it was to them.

A later survey, sent to the same engineers after an interim of several weeks (so that they would not feel that the staff of the research library was 'harassing' them or asking too much of them), asked the engineers to determine how much time they saved by having the research library on site. In other words, to state how much time it would take for them to obtain elsewhere the informa- tion they accessed through the company's research library. The responses, dramatic in hours alone, when multiplied by the average hourly wage for the engineers established some rather phenomenal financial values for the worth of the research library. In terms of hard, cold cash, it was proven to be a valuable asset.

By now you know the end of the story. The utilities company did, within a few months' time, go into a massive downsizing effort, and drastic staff and service reductions were put in place in every department of the organization . . . except in the research library. On the other hand, the corporate library across town ceased to exist, and its former users hardly noticed it was gone.

. . . What would have happened if the library manager at the utilities company had waited to be 'invited' to participate in an evaluation of the library and its services, if she had been reactive instead of proactive? Surely there's no mystery here, and the moral to this tale is not a hidden one. ('A Tale of Two Corporate Libraries,' pp. 7–8)

The story illustrates some of the cost/benefit analysis and value added concepts described by Miriam A. Drake in her 1987 article, in which she created a model which provides important guidance for information services managers. By describing four levels of service commonly provided in academic libraries (from the basic, almost self-service model, through access, document delivery, and the packaging of the information), Drake was able to demonstrate that the cost/benefit analysis of the information service could be based upon such things as user cost, opportunity cost, the focus of the information transaction (e.g., whether materials-focused or client-focused), and the level of added value inherent in the transaction. Drake's criteria represented useful measures which senior management and (in this case) university administrators could use for evaluating information services (Drake, p. [17]). Without question, such measures are not only effective, they are required for the successful allocation of resources required for the management of an information services agency or operation, regardless of the parent organization or community of which it is a part.

Staff

Finally, in determining the organizational structure of an information services unit or operation, attention must be given to the staffing needs of the unit. Not only are such concerns as the selection, hiring, and training of staff essential components in the well-being of an information services department, such 'organizational' issues as compatibility, loyalty, and service values must be addressed as well. Managerial effort is required to ensure that information workers understand the role of information in the parent organization or community, and all staff in the information services section must be united in their commitment to the highest standards of information delivery for their constituent users. Of course conflicts will arise, and while ethical and moral issues cannot be compromised, in the best-managed information services units the resolution of these conflicts will include a consideration of corporate or organizational values.

Think about, for example, a real estate firm in which the corporate library, procuring external sales and marketing information for senior management, is operated as a discrete unit. On the other hand, much of the information it provides could be of great value to the company's sales force if it could be connected with certain sales and marketing reports generated internally and controlled through the corporate records department. A staff member in the corporate library has conceived and developed a system for matching these separate sets of information, and while MIS staff is generally enthusiastic about the idea and encourages further development, leading to beta testing of the product, the manager of the corporate library is cool to the concept. He argues, with some justification, that the organizational culture at the company does not encourage such 'maverick' behavior amongst it staff, and without specific direction from senior management and a commitment of support for the project, the library manager will not cooperate and is naturally unenthusiastic about any participation by his staff member (who had the idea in the first place!). What needs to be remembered here is that information staff does impact upon organizational behavior within the information services unit. While it seems like a positive thing – and it is – to develop innovative behavior in staff, it also must be recognized, as this information services manager has recognized, that such behavior is irregular within the organization at large. On the other hand, managerial responsibility could, if the information services manager were so inclined, lead to a changed attitude on the part of senior management if he, as an advocate for his 'maverick' staff member, were willing to risk some organizational disappointment if he and his staff obtained senior management's support and then failed in the endeavor. In either case, it is the manager of the information services unit who has responsibility for the department's success and he, recognizing the risks involved, must decide whether or not to take them.

The achievement of power and influence within the parent organization or community, and the success of the information services operation in achieving its goals within the organization or community are connected directly to the management of the unit. Decisions about levels of service, resource allocation, staff qualifications, effectiveness measures, and similar issues seriously affect how well the information services unit is able to perform. The unit's performance – and perceptions about that performance – are now the determining factors in establishing value for information services within the parent organization or community. If the information staff does its job, and does it well, the battle is half won. From this point, it is a relatively easy task for managers to look at 'enhancing' the value of the information services unit within the parent organization or community. Once a high quality of information services delivery *and* the perception throughout the organization that high-quality services are being delivered have been achieved, all of the other components in this now not-so-complicated process fall into place. From now on, to achieve that enhancement, information services managers look to their own leadership skills, to a raised organizational awareness about information services, and to active participation in planning for future information and organizational needs.

References

Albrecht, Karl. *At America's Service: How Corporations can Revolutionize the Way they Treat their Customers*. Homewood, IL: Dow Jones-Irwin, 1988.

Asantewa, Doris. *Strategic Planning Basics for Special Libraries*. Washington, DC: Special Libraries Association, 1992.

Bauer, Charles K. 'Managing management.' *Special Libraries*. 71 (4), April, 1980.

Drake, Miriam A. 'Value of the information professional: cost/benefit analysis.' *President's Task Force on the Value of the Information Professional, Final Report, Preliminary Study, June 10, 1987*. Washington, DC: Special Libraries Association, 1987.

Ferguson, Elizabeth, and Mobley, Emily R. *Special Libraries at Work*. Hamden, CT: The Shoe String Press, 1984.

Ferriero, David S. and Wilding, Thomas L. 'Scanning the environment in strategic planning.' *Masterminding Tomorrow's Information - Creative Strategies for the '90s: Professional Papers from the 82nd Annual Conference of the Special Libraries Association, San Antonio, TX, June 8-13, 1991*. Washington, DC: Special Libraries Association, 1991.

Harps, Leslie. 'Using Customer Service to Keep Subscribers.' A Presentation to the Newsletter Publishers Association, Washington, DC. January 21, 1992 (unpublished).

Jones, Cathy. 'The information interview: It's the staff - Catherine A. Jones talks about LC's Congressional Reference Division.' *InfoManage: The International Management Newsletter for the Information Services Executive*. 1 (2), January, 1994.

Labovitz, Judy. 'Managing a special library.' *Journal of Library Administration*. 6 (3), Fall, 1985.

Manning, Helen. 'The corporate librarian: great return on investment.' *President's Task Force on the Value of the Information Professional*. Washington, DC: Special Libraries Association, 1987.

Matarazzo, James M., Prusak, Laurence, and Gauthier, Michael R. *Valuing Corporate Libraries: A Survey of Senior Managers*. Washington, DC: Special Libraries Association, 1990.

Mount, Ellis. *Special Libraries and Information Centers: An Introductory Text*. Washington, DC: Special Libraries Association, 1991.

Newsome, James, and McInerney, Claire. 'Environmental scanning and the information manager.' *Special Libraries*. 81 (4), Fall, 1990.

O'Donnell, William S. 'The vulnerable corporate special library/information center: minimizing the risks.' *Special Libraries*. 67, April, 1976.

Palmer, Richard Phillips, and Varnet, Harvey. *How to Manage Information: A Systems Approach*. Phoenix, AZ: Oryx Press, 1990.

Palmour, Vernon El, et al. *A Planning Process for Public Libraries*. Chicago: American Library Association, 1980.

Sager, Donald J. *Managing the Public Library*. Boston, MA: G.K. Hall, 1989.

Strable, Edward G. 'Special libraries: how are they different?' *Illinois Libraries*. 62, March, 1980.

Szilagyi, Andrew D., Jr. *Management and Performance*. New York: Scott, Foresman and Company, 1988.

Talcott, Ann. 'Managing electronic libraries.' *Managing the Electronic Library: Papers of the 1982 Conference of the Library Management Division of the Special Libraries Association*, edited by Michael Koenig. New York: Special Libraries Association, 1983.

'A tale of two corporate libraries.' *InfoManage: The International Management Newsletter for the Information Services Executive*. 1 (3), February, 1994.

Turock, Betty J. 'Valuing information services.' *The Bottom Line Reader: A Financial Handbook for Librarians*. New York: Neal-Schuman, 1990.

Waldron, Helen J. 'The business of running a special library.' *Special Libraries*. 62, February, 1971.

White, Herbert S. *Managing the Special Library*. White Plains, NY: Knowledge Industry Publications, 1984.

Wright, Craig. 'Corporate records management and the librarian.' *Special Libraries*. 82 (4), Fall, 1991.

Chapter Seven

Leading, controlling, and managing change

Leadership and management

Excellence in a specialized library, corporate information center, records management department, computer services section, or indeed, in any other information services unit in an organization or community is characterized by the presence of an individual who truly *leads* the unit. She or he literally creates a culture that enables and motivates the unit, through its staff, to fulfill its mission. Creating such a culture is a management responsibility, as Judy Labovitz has described:

> If the library [staff members] work as a team, if they like what they do, if the staff is competent and communication is good, a set of shared values will emerge that will form the basis of a 'library personality'. (Labovitz, p. 8)

The 'culture' is built first, of course, on the service provided by the unit and its staff, but it is a fairly short step from excellent services to a 'culture' or 'personality' of excellence. For example, in one fairly large engineering company, the staff in the corporate research center became known not only for its dependability in providing the information its users needed, but for the ease with which that information was delivered. The research center was characterized by many engineers throughout the company as 'the least bureaucratic' department, the 'easiest to use' unit, the 'most responsive' department, and so forth, a characterization which did much to increase the research center's viability and value for its users and for the company as a whole. Upon investigation, of course, it was easy to see why the department was so described. The manager of the department was a woman whose combined leadership and managerial skills went straight to the core of the unit's objective, to provide the information that the engineers needed in order to do their work. An energetic woman with a scientific background of her own, married to one of the engineers who worked for the company, this department head recognized that the unit's information customers could not afford to deal with a bureaucracy. She hired and trained people who shared her own information values, who delighted in the challenges of information delivery, and who accepted, with her, that their success in the organizational structure was directly connected to the success with which they performed their duties. With these kinds of influences at work, it is no surprise that the corporate research center in this engineering company is acknowledged with pride throughout the firm.

In thinking about enhancing an information services operation within a parent organization or community and about how that unit can acquire influence and power, John Gardner's basic definition comes into play. Leadership, he says, is 'the process of persuasion and example by which an individual (or leadership team) induces a group to take action that is in accord with the leader's purpose or the shared purposes of all' (Gardner, p. 6). The manager of the information services unit has a specific purpose in mind: he wants the organization to recognize the value of the information unit, and to incorporate it and its staff's expertise into the organizational mainstream. What this person does, in effect, is to use his leadership skills not only in his interactions with the people who report to him, that is, with his own staff, but with the people to whom he reports, as well as with the customers for whom the unit provides information. By persuading these groups, however subtly, to come around to his point of view about the value of information, and by influencing them so that they themselves are conveying to others this same point of view, the manager of the information services unit is successfully combining leadership and managerial skills.

There is, of course, the on-going debate about people who are or are not 'born' leaders, but for our purposes, the distinction matters little and the subject is, in fact, a non-issue. Even the most basic level of information services provision requires an ability to understand the needs of users, to determine from them how they will use the information they seek, and to work with them in establishing the best and most effective routes to that information. Thus even the simplest information services transaction can – or should – require leadership ability on the part of the information worker. When those services are raised to a higher plane, the 'built-in', so to speak, leadership requirements of the information interaction become even more evident, and the information worker automatically finds himself or herself in a leadership position in dealing with the query. As to who possesses leadership characteristics and who does not, Peter Drucker has the answer: 'There are simply no such things as "leadership traits" or "leadership characteristics". Of course, some people are better leaders than others. By and large, though, we are talking about skills that perhaps cannot be taught but they can be learned by most of us. True, some people genuinely cannot learn the skills. They may not be important to them; or they'd rather be followers. But most of us can learn them.' (Drucker, p. 18). And learn them we do, for every information worker has to bring to the information transaction at least a modicum of leadership ability, if he or she is going to be successful in bringing together the information customer and the information that that person is seeking.

Leadership qualities

By as early as 1940, Chester Barnard had identified and prioritized five 'qualities of leaders', which he expounded upon in presentations for the US Army and at the Harvard School of Business Administration (as it was called then). Athough Barnard was concerned that 'leadership' was becoming confused with what he called '*preeminence*' or '*extraordinary usefulness*', he was also determined to bring leadership, as a subject of study, into the business management discussions of his day, and he went to some lengths to clear up this misunderstanding about what he saw as a 'double meaning' for the concept of leadership. In discussing leadership in its connection to management theory, it is appropriate to recognize that there is, perhaps, a double meaning which can cause confusion. Barnard recognized this double meaning, and noted that in the view of many, 'a leading writer, artist, pianist, mathematician, or scientist exemplifies leadership substantially as does an executive or leader of an organization' (Barnard, p. 81). While the term 'to lead' can be defined as characterizing a person who excels or is preeminent in this or that field of endeavor, it also means, as Barnard pointed out, 'to guide others, to govern their activities, to be head of an organization or some part of it, to hold command'. In this context, the 'active qualities' which Barnard identified as characteristic of leadership can be appropriately studied by information services executives. His list follows, with excerpted remarks which Barnard included in his presentations:

> Vitality and endurance . . . promote and permit the unremitting acquirement of exceptional experience and knowledge which in general underlies extraordinary personal capacity for leadership, . . . [they are] usually an element in personal attractiveness or force which is a great aid to persuasiveness, . . . [and] leadership often involves prolonged periods of work and extreme tension without relief, when failure to endure may mean permanent inability to lead.
>
> Decisiveness . . . [is] the characteristic of leaders I think most to be noted. It depends upon a propensity or willingness to decide and a capacity to do so.
>
> Persuasiveness . . . [without which] all other qualities may become ineffective . . . involves a *sense* or understanding of the point of view, the interests, and the conditions of those to be persuaded.
>
> Responsibility, the emotional condition that gives an individual a sense of acute dissatisfaction because of failure to do what he feels he is morally bound to do or because of doing what he thinks he is morally bound not to do, in particular concrete situations. Such dissatisfaction he will avoid; and therefore his behavior, if he is 'responsible' and if his beliefs or sense of what is right are known, can be approximately relied upon.

> Intellectual capacity. . . . Intellectual abilities of high order may achieve preeminent usefulness. They are sometimes an important element in leadership but not sufficient to maintain it. However, as a differential factor – that is, other qualities being granted and adequate – intellectual capacity is of unquestioned importance, and especially in the age in which complex techniques and elaborate technologies are among the conditions of leadership. (Barnard, pp. 93–95)

Indeed, if Barnard had had any concept of the 'elaborate' technologies with which the information services manager would be confronted at the end of the twentieth century, he would probably have put his requirement for intellectual capacity at the top of his list, and he would have been anticipating the very component of information services management that brings out the best in today's information leaders. For them, it is the very 'elaborateness' of the technology which excites and stretches the managerial role. And it is that very excitement and intellectual endeavor which brings the information services manager into a position of leadership within the organization or community of which her information operation is a part.

Think about, for example, an experienced information services manager who is about to take a new job with another company. It is a software development company, only twelve years old, but it is successful and while there has never been a corporate information center before, one is now needed. The Vice-President for Corporate Development assured this woman, as she was being recruited for the position, that what the firm needed was a leader, a person who could, in the original sense of the term, 'lead' the company into the establishment and utilization of a dynamic, proactive information services operation. As she described the various interviews that led to her being offered the position, the woman reported, without being aware that she was doing so, that the company's executive who interviewed her had in fact been seeking the very 'qualities' which Barnard had identified a half century before. In organizing the new corporate information center, much planning, organization and political negotiation would be required, and the job would, at least temporarily, take on a life of its own, to the exclusion of much else in her personal and private life (vitality and endurance). Experience would be required, for the new information center would be solidly funded, and the recommendations for using those resources would be hers (decisiveness). On the other hand, the company, as a whole, and particularly some of the senior managers, were not entirely committed to the new service. Neither were some of the company's engineers and researchers, who were accustomed to providing their own information, however inefficiently, from resources immediately at hand. The new manager for the information center would be required to convince them that the very existence of the center was in their best interests (persuasiveness). Considering the resources – financial, human, material, etc. – at her disposal, the new information services manager would clearly be bound morally and ethically to use those resources reliably and responsibly, that is, to display the 'stability of behavior' that Barnard referred to (responsibility). Finally, because of the nature of the company, the chronological point at which she found herself in her career, and the particular age in which we live, she would be required to master, or at least hire people who could master, a great diversity of 'complex techniques and elaborate technologies' (intellectual capacity). To perform successfully in the job, she would be required to be a leader/manager, and to excel in her performance of the duties of a leader/manager.

Several authorities have distinguished between managers, who see their work as directing others, and leader/managers, whose role combines direction with what might be referred to as simply 'inspiration'. Abraham Zaleznik, for example, took this approach:

> Managers tend to adopt impersonal, if not passive, attitudes toward goals. Managerial goals arise out of necessities rather than desires and, therefore, are deeply embedded in their organization's history and culture. . . . To get people to accept solutions to problems, managers continually need to coordinate and balance opposing views. Interestingly enough, this type of work has much in common with what diplomats do . . . managers aim to shift balances of power toward solutions acceptable as compromises among conflicting values.
>
> Leaders work in the opposite direction. Where managers act to limit choices, leaders develop fresh approaches to long-standing problems and open issues to new options. To be effective, leaders must project their ideas onto images that excite people and only then develop choices that give those images substance. (Zaleznik, pp. 127–129)

John Gardner has identified six differences between managers and leader/managers, and for information services executives, these distinctions can be significant (Gardner, p. 8). In the first place, leader/managers 'think longer term – beyond the day's crises, beyond the quarterly report, beyond the horizon'. For the information services manager, attention to immediate duties is of course an important and required activity, but he has been made a manager because of what he *can* do, not necessarily because of what he does day-to-day. Therefore, a considerable amount of energy, for the leader/manager in the information services unit, is needed to think about future operations and to plan for them, whether in terms of services, technology, or any of the other many components that contribute to the successful delivery of information to constituent users.

Leader/managers are also distinguished, according to Gardner, because 'they look beyond the unit they are heading and grasp its relationship to larger realities – the larger organization of which they are a part, conditions external to the organization, global trends'. The information services executive, if he or she is to succeed in enhancing the information services operation within the organization, must fully understand and exploit the organization's and *its* leaders' goals, aspirations, and desires. If, for example, a manufacturer's major competitor is considering the development of a 'fringe' product, the information services staff at the manufacturer has an obligation to be researching the same 'fringe' product, not only for competitive reasons but because the industry, if the competitor is successful, will be impacted and the manufacturer does not want to be left behind in the development of these new products.

The third of the distinctions which Gardner identified between managers and leader/managers is that the latter 'reach and influence constituents beyond their jurisdictions, beyond boundaries'. The concept can be implemented internally when, for example, in a company in which the librarians provide information for specialists in corporate law, they are also aware of what is happening in the real estate section of the firm, or externally, as when the corporate archivists of several petroleum companies, all located within the same geographical region, meet on a regular basis to discuss and develop new techniques for better serving their individual client groups.

Gardner found that leader/managers tend to 'put heavy emphasis on the intangibles of vision, values and motivation and understand intuitively the non-rational and unconscious elements in the leader-consituent interaction'. Picture the challenges ahead for the manager of the new corporate information center at the software development firm described earlier. In such an environment, she would be foolish to attempt to build a 'traditional library' organizational structure for the firm. The primary customers, being scientists and technical workers, are not going to be interested in such a concept, and as she hires staff, she is wise to look for innovative, individualistic types (who of course understand the value of team work) who could be hired specifically to look upon the challenges of the new situation as opportunities for utilizing their kind of thinking. It will be her task to bring order out of the chaos, but the ultimate product – the up-and-running information center – will be far more useful to its constituent customers if it has been designed with their needs and their 'culture' in mind.

At the same time, the information services manager, if she is a leader/manager, will be able to deal with both the 'traditionalists' and the 'techies', for that is her brief. As Gardner points out, the leader/managers 'have the political skill to cope with the conflicting requirements of multiple constituencies', and her success in the creation of the information center will reflect her ability to determine which levels of service will be providing for the various consituent units that will be accessing information through her operation.

Finally, Gardner recognizes that the leader/managers 'think in terms of renewal. The routine manager tends to accept the structure and processes as they exist. The leader or leader/manager seeks the revisions of process and structure required by ever-changing reality.' Well put. For the information services executive, in this time of continual change, and as information services as a specific branch of the service sector advances into the twenty-first century, constant renewal is a given. In the past, managers have allowed themselves to pretend that vital components of the workplace, such things as staff, the economy, profits, relations with customers and suppliers, and the like, would stay the same, but those ideas, if they were ever true, are certainly today nothing but sweet illusions. Nothing is staying the same; all is changing. The successful information services leader/manager, recognizing the value of change, its desirability and its inevitability (as will be discussed below) will use change to enhance his or her own leadership position within the parent organization or community. It is the only way to go, and the leader/manager, by denying it, will only, ultimately, jeopardize the work he or she has been charged to do.

So the question becomes not *whether* information services managers can be leaders, but *how* they can acquire leadership skills if they do not have them. Nowadays, there is no question that those responsible for the delivery of information services and products must bring to their organizations more than a mere knowledge of information and management. If they are going to succeed, as supervisors of the people who report to them, as peers with others at their managerial level, and, certainly, as promoters and advocates for information services to senior management, leadership ability is required. The skills themselves are best described by Warren Bennis, who recognized that leadership, in a managerial environment, is best defined through the people who are providing leadership. In every organization or community, and certainly in any information services operation, these people, according to Bennis, are those:

> . . . Who are able to express themselves fully . . . they know who they are, what their strengths and weaknesses are, and how to fully deploy their strengths and compensate for their weaknesses . . . they know what they want, why they want it, and how to communicate what they want to others, in order to gain their cooperation and support. . . . They know how to achieve their goals. (Bennis, p. 3)

Control and accountability

To ensure that the work in the information services unit gets done, the manager of the unit is responsible for establishing authority, responsibility, and accountability relationships. While much has been written about the so-called 'flat' managerial structure, and while many companies and organizations have excelled and will continue to excel in implementing such open relationships for the successful achievement of their organizational objectives, the requirements for control and accountability in any enterprise will necessitate a certain level of responsibility for a set group of leaders within the organization. Although writing in another context, John Rollwagen caught the essential essence of this idea when he wrote:

> A business, of course, is anything but democratic. Though it's not a dictatorship, people unquestioningly understand that somebody needs to be in charge;

> somebody ultimately needs to decide which single purpose the company will pursue. The secret of business, especially these days, is to focus relentlessly on your unfair advantage – the thing you do that others don't. Mindful of that focus, you decide on specific objectives and on the division of labor needed to achieve them. Plenty of debate may precede the setting of those goals, but in the end everyone signs on. Which makes business an essentially exclusionary enterprise, not an inclusionary one. Anybody is welcome to join as long as he or she agrees with exactly what we're for. If you don't agree, please don't come; go do something else. (Rollwagen, p. 25)

In the information services field, one of the unpleasant surprises for new employees at entry-level positions is the wide disparity between the egalitarianism of their graduate training and the harsh realities of the workplace. Rollwagen is correct when he states that life in the business world is not ruled by dictatorship, but one learns early on that authority must be established, and in the management of an information services unit, while every effort can be made to create an 'open' managerial arrangement, complete with management teams, participatory management, quality circles and the like, all of them necessary and important components of the management picture, the fact of the matter is that every managerial unit, including the information services department, must incorporate into its organization high productivity goals, together with evaluative methods for ensuring that productivity standards are kept high.

For the information services manager, the basic steps in the control process are the establishment of performance standards, the measuring of performance against the standards, and the establishment and implementation of whatever corrective action is required to bring performance up to the standards which were established in the first place. An example can be found in an agricultural research institute, where the flow time between the receipt of a request for a technical report, filed onsite, and the delivery of the report had been established, through experience and through negotiations with clients, as 48 hours or less. Having determined that the timeframe was realistic, and noting that 78 percent of all reports were indeed delivered within 48 hours, the manager of the technical report storage center took it upon herself to determine why the other 22 percent of the requests were delivered late. For some reason, report requests originating from a remote site were being responded to like all other requests, but the documents themselves were being delivered through regular mail service, rather than through the organization's own courier service (which was the method of delivery for requests from all other remote sites). Corrective action was called for – the utilization of the organization's courier service – and performance was significantly improved. In this case, the manager of the technical report storage facility was able to implement control through the implementation of basic measurement procedures.

Part of any organization's control activity has to do with the evaluation of individual and group performance and productivity, and the information services unit is no exception. If the department is to be seen as a critical entity in the work of the parent organization or community, the work that is produced in the department must be evaluated and measured in the same terms, and using the same language, as other units of the enterprise. It has long been a tradition that information services providers (librarians, records managers, archivists, etc.) were seen as 'providing a service', but that measuring the activity required for providing the 'service' was not necessary. That is no longer the case. Senior management in all organizations want output and effectiveness measures documented, critical analysis of not only how many transactions take place, but how useful those transactions are or were to the customers who initiated them.

The information services field as a whole is beginning to look seriously at evaluation and measurement of work, a point made by José-Marie Griffiths and Donald W. King, two leaders in the profession who have made special efforts in this direction. Introducing their manual for evaluating information centers and services, Griffiths and King offered solid reasons for the introduction of performance measures:

> Institutions of all kinds worldwide are undergoing intensive scrutiny in terms of their performance and effectiveness, we believe properly so. It is no longer accepted as matter of fact that information centers are necessary or that all services are needed. Information centers are undergoing increasingly strong competition for funds within their companies, educational institutions, government agencies or other organizations. . . . Unfortunately, many information centers are not well prepared to meet this competition. They typically do not measure or keep data that are useful for making a compelling case for themselves in a highly competitive environment. (Griffiths and King, p. 3)

Griffiths and King have identified several 'themes' having to do with measurement and evaluation which are germane to the discussion of performance standards in an information services environment. Taken together, these ideas constitute a useful and provocative starting point for the information services manager who is seeking to incorporate productivity and service measurement into his department's work and, thus, into the department's connection, so to speak, with the other departments and sections of the organization. Griffiths and King suggest the following:

- Evaluation must have a purpose; it must not be an end in itself.

- Without the potential for some action, there is no need to evaluate.

- Evaluation must be more than descriptive; rather evaluation must take into account relationships between operational performance and effects on the users and organizations being served.

- Evaluation should be a communications tool where feedback to and from staff and users is unimpeded.

- Evaluation should not be sporadic in nature, but rather should be considered as an ongoing management tool supported by an ongoing system of measures or management information system.

- Ongoing evaluation should provide a means for continual monitoring, diagnosis and change.

- Ongoing evaluation should be dynamic in nature, in that evaluation measures, models and methods must reflect new knowledge and changes in the operational, user and organizational environment. (Griffiths and King, p. 3)

If we want to examine these evaluation 'themes' more closely, we might look at an example from the theatrical community, specifically the corporate information center serving a large talent agency. In an attempt to monitor ongoing work, senior management has recommended that all departmental managers look at productivity in the units for which they are responsible. The corporate information center, which is composed of a specialized library, a records management unit, and a corporate archives section, is under the jurisdiction of the Vice-President for Information Services, who is also responsible for internal automation services and MIS. Two people report to her, the Director, Corporate Information Center, and the Director, Computer Services.

The evaluation process is taken up quickly and expeditiously by the Director of the Corporate Information Center, who sees it as an opportunity to raise awareness throughout the agency about the type of work done in the center and the high quality of the staff who report to him. Thus the evaluation, for this manager, has a 'purpose', as Griffiths and King have recommended. The Director of Computer Services is a little less enthusiastic, for she and her staff cannot see any purpose in evaluating and measuring the work done in their department, and in fact any attempt to quantify their work, she feels, would be counterproductive and require more effort that it would be worth.

The Director of the Corporate Information Center sees a potential for action, for by raising awareness about what his department offers, he and his staff will be able to provide services for more people, a goal that was established early on by him and by senior management. Similarly, he considers an evaluation a useful tool because it will not be 'merely descriptive'. It will point out how the three units of his department work as one, and his staff's ability to deal with all queries, regardless of whether they are for external information through the library or for internal information culled from the agency's current records or the corporate archives. In all cases, the evaluation will establish how the various types of information are interconnected within the company.

Part of the process, of course, is gathering data from other staff in the agency, the 'customers' who use the information services unit, and from the Corporate Information Center's own staff. By having open presentations, interviews and the like, the evaluation does away with the kind of secrecy that can harm such an effort, and in fact by talking openly about some of the company's information concerns, information services staff – and particularly the managers – will be in a position to review and, hopefully, bring in innovative and creative solutions to users' information problems.

By organizing an evaluative exercise as part of the department's regular tasks, the Director of the Corporate Information Center will, in fact, be establishing an ongoing measurement process which, among other things, will permit the department to monitor and report continuous improvement, one of the basic ingredients in the evaluative process. In organizing and setting up an ongoing evaluation, complete with 'continual monitoring and diagnosis', as Griffiths and King phrase it, management in the information services section is recognizing that its role in the organization is a critical one requiring an aggressive, communicative and entrepreneurial approach to intra-organizational activity.

Finally, in using Griffiths and King's guidelines, the Director of the Corporate Information Center will look for different models and measures, after a while not being satisfied with those he started with, since so much will change during the process. He will work with other managers throughout the agency to determine what methods they are using and together, as members of the same corporate team, they will devise new approaches when needed.

Change management

Resistance to change can be the primary barrier to effective information services management in any organization or community, and the information services manager must give attention to those parts of change management that influence the work that she and her staff do. In this day and age, the frank acceptance of change as both desirable and inevitable is a basic requirement for the successful provision of information services and products. At the same time, an effective change-management program can play a critical role in establishing the success of an information services unit or department within an organization or community.

Susan C. Curzon has pointed out that the change process has various decision points, and as a first step, to deal with a more conservative approach first, it would be a responsible action for the manager of the information services unit to assess the consequences of any proposed change before proceeding with the change. Putting the brakes on an enthusiastic 'change-for-change's-sake' situation is better done earlier than later, which Curzon notes:

One of the characteristics of change is that it can appear more urgent and valuable than it really is. Change can be exciting, and while it is human nature to go toward that which is new and different, this does not necessarily make for sound organizational decisions. (Curzon, p. 25)

While innovation and entrepreneurial thinking are called for in every information services organization, and can certainly lead to better information products and services for more information customers, Curzon's questions about the 'consequences of change', as she calls it, are valuable and provide a realistic platform from which to assess proposed change (Curzon, p. 25). Using them as a point of departure for a hypothetical situation, we might look at managing change in a case study.

In a large trade association which represents the developers and manufacturers of equipment used in the processing of chemical waste, the senior management and elected leadership of the organization, including its board of directors, has voted to make its primary function one of providing 'timely, convenient' information to its members. Consequently, an enthusiastic and well-qualified information scientist has been hired to develop information products which will be offered, as a benefit of membership, to the scientists and manufacturers who belong to the organization.

The association has a standards unit, which collects standards from various agencies and organizations and distributes them, in paper format, to members upon request. After a year of study, the information scientist is proposing that the association offer its standards electronically, both online and in a CD-ROM product. The organization's staff, which has heretofore been a fairly reactive entity for membership requests, is suddenly thrown into great disarray, since the change, as proposed, will require a total restructuring of processes and procedures. In the standards unit, especially, the resistance is very strong, because the 25-member standards staff, following an organizational pattern established in 1952, feels that it is doing its work well, since it successfully meets the performance standards of its original mission.

With the enactment, by the leadership of the organization, of what is, in effect, a new mission for the organization, the following questions must be considered (Curzon's questions are highlighted):

Is the change legitimate? If the association's constitution and by-laws permit the leadership of the association to change the focus of the organizational mission statement, the change is legitimate. In fact, in this situation, the leadership is only doing what the leadership in any organization must do, and that is to provide the most up-to-date methods for responding to members' needs. With a mechanism created in the fifties, the association, while perhaps meeting the demand, is not doing it in the most efficient and effective way.

Is the change a priority? Only the leadership of the organization can answer this question, but apparently there has been enough interest on the part of the membership (who are, after all, scientists and businesspeople who, in their other efforts, must utilize modern methods) to generate this move toward a change.

Is the change worth the price? For the membership, the value of the change is a different matter. Unless they will be expected to pay much higher financial fees for the changed service (which, as proposed, will be a benefit of membership, just as it is with the delivery of paper copies of the standards), the costs of the change are not a consideration.

What are the limits of the organization? Again, this is a question that only the leadership can answer, but obviously if the information scientist has been hired to design products and services for the membership, the financial or organizational limitations have already been taken into consideration before the change is proposed.

What are the parameters of change? Such matters as the establishment of parallel standards delivery, both on paper and electronically, must be built into the change, unless the association's leadership has already determined, through member surveys and the like, that all of its members are ready to receive standards electronically. Similarly, other parameters, such as staff competencies, start-up funding and the like will have to be looked at.

Is the change consistent with the organization? Apparently, the leadership of the organization is prepared to offer the new information product to the membership, so studies have been done to determine that the change is appropriate for the organization. Were this an organization in which the electronic delivery of information products was not appropriate to the members' needs and interests, of course, a different approach would be required.

Is the change needed? Certainly the innovative information scientist has determined that most – if not all – of the scientists and manufacturers who are members of the organization would be satisfied by the electronic delivery of standards information, and more than likely has also determined that some members are in fact obtaining this information electronically from other, competitive organizations.

Has the organization as a whole been considered? If there are pockets of resistance in the membership, and certainly with the resisting staff, efforts must be made to assure them that the change will enable the association to better meet its obligations for achieving its mission, certainly its mission as now re-defined.

Obviously, a major component of change management is dealing with the people involved, which has been pointed out by Tom G. Watson in a useful essay in 1983. Many workers in the organization are going to be disconcerted by the change process, and Watson suggests why:

> . . . People tend to develop subjective hunches about whether change in the workplace will be harmful or helpful to them in their own job situations and [they] will thus formulate their attitude about and behavior toward the change accordingly. (Watson, p. 90)

Watson goes on to point out, of course, that if the employee expects the change to bring advantages to him and his work, he will support the change. Conversely, if he expects the change to be 'bad', he will not support it and will, given the opportunity, do what he can to thwart the change. Finally, the worst case scenario, according to Watson, is if he has not been brought into the change process, and is in a 'state of considerable anxiety', as Watson describes it, about possible outcomes, then he will almost certainly resist the change.

Watson makes another important observation:

> Another factor which change agents in all types of organizations . . . have failed fully to appreciate is that a person who has worked in one job in a particular organization for a long time quite likely has come to identify his job and his job performance with the kind of person he perceives himself to be. (Watson, p. 91)

Certainly this characteristic of the employee applies to the information practitioner. In delivering information products and services, the information employee is called upon to play a variety of roles, including that of advisor, educator, counselor, navigator, and, frequently, arbitrator, for the information customer is coming to the worker to have an information problem solved. Regardless of the worker's true skills and abilities for performing these information tasks, in the eye of the customer he or she is the expert, the person who can deliver the goods. As a result, the information worker is more often than not called upon to utilize creative, intuitive techniques for providing the information and, naturally, the creativity will break down from time to time. Nevertheless, the information worker, whether he or she is a librarian, records clerk, archivist or any of the other myriad employees in the service sector who provide information, becomes accustomed to being the 'expert' and is very uncomfortable with the idea of giving up that role to which he has, unwittingly or not, been assigned by his or her 'public'. When confronted with change (no matter how good the change is for the organization or the information services unit of which he or she is a part), this employee is going to resist. For the information services manager, employee counseling of the highest order is mandated, and the manager must expend much energy and effort in bringing the employee around to recognizing the validity of the change.

The structure of the unit, too, has much to do with the success of the change process. Rosabeth Moss Kanter identified those companies in which innovation and entrepreneurial thinking were encouraged and was able to connect their success in the area of change mangement with organizational structure. Surely these same characteristics apply to the various subunits – such as an information services department – of these organizations as well:

> The highest proportion of entrepreneurial accomplishments is found in the companies that are least segmented and segmentalist, companies that instead have integrative structures and cultures emphasizing pride, commitment, collaboration, and teamwork. The companies producing more managerial entrepreneurs have more complex structures that link people in multiple ways and encourage them to 'do what needs to be done', within strategically guided limits, rather than confining themselves to the letter of their job. They are encouraged to take initiative and to behave cooperatively. (Kanter, p. 178)

The difficulties the scientific trade association is encountering have much to do with the organizational structure. Although managerial staff, elected leadership and the directors have all gone on record supporting a new mission for the organization, and although it *appears* that the membership at large is ready (even anxious) to accept a new direction for the organization, those pockets of resistance described earlier can be attributed to a lack of communication or commitment, on the part of the organization's leadership, to convey the need for the change to the more recalcitrant people who might be affected by the change. Assumptions were made, but in fact, in this case study, it seems clear that some sort of promotional or 'good-will' campaign might have been initiated to determine that all stakeholders in the information delivery process were willing to 'buy into' the new mission.

To be fair about it, however, there are few organizations which initiate change – at whatever level – with such sensitivity. In most cases, somewhere among the stakeholders a decision is made to enact change, and the decision is carried forth to the remaining members of the community. Nevertheless, for those information services managers who are dealing with change on a regular basis (and all of us are, or will be), it is comforting to know that there are ways to enact change without totally disrupting the flow of information (or life in the workplace), a point made by Kanter when she reported some of her observations:

> Life is by no means perfect in the innovating companies. Certainly not all managers have the same access to power, and systems promoting innovativeness also bring with them a new set of problems of managing participation, ambiguity, and complexity. But if life is not perfect, at least the tools exist to use to make corrective changes. (Kanter, p. 179)

The information services manager who enacts change successfully will make a serious effort to bring those tools into the workplace, using them to work with his or her staff to support the change effort, and not defeat it.

For information services practitioners thinking about change management, and how the change process – when it works – relates to power and influence within the organization for the information services unit, Dalziel and Schoonover offer good advice. What needs to happen, they suggest, is the development of an 'ethic of change', which, in today's workplace, is required for the successful achievement of the organizational mission and within it, of course, departmental or other subunit missions as well. Change is a part of life, of the workplace, and the acceptance of change as both inevitable and desirable will lead to positive and fruitful relationships on the job. Just as Kanter has suggested, Dalziel and Schoonover recognize that 'the best leaders make change an organization value by modeling, teaching, reinforcing, and refining the principles of the change model in all day-to-day operations' (Dalziel and Schoonover, p. 156). If the information services unit in the organization is going to be perceived by others, especially the decision makers and other information stakeholders, as valuable to the organization, and not just as a stand-alone services unit, three factors prevail, as Dalziel and Schoonover state them:

> Change leaders devote as much time to dealing with human and organizational issues as with technical issues. (Dalziel and Schoonover, p. 156)

In the association/standards example given earlier, the innovative information scientist, his manager and, indeed, the entire leadership of the organization must be united in their efforts to establish for the dissenting staff and members the value of the electronic distribution of standards information. This means that the human fears and concerns of the 'nay-sayers' must be addressed, considered and given attention to, since these are people who will be affected by the change, despite the fact that it is an *organizational* change which is being implemented.

Change leaders must 'make problem solving the norm'. Although it is now a cliché to say so, everyone reacts to change differently. Reactions throughout the organization – and the implementation of the change process itself – will set in motion an abundance of problem situations, and the effective information services manager will recognize them as such and make immediate and conscientious efforts to deal with them as problems, not ignore them or postpone dealing with them because he or she is 'uncomfortable' with problems. Problem solving is part of change management, and it can be, with the right attitude on the part of managers, a rewarding and gratifying component of the process.

Change leaders recognize the value of openness about information, are comfortable with it, and, as Dalziel and Schoonover say, 'allow information to flow freely, so that problems can be solved'. It is up to the information services manager to determine that the organization's policies about the flow of information will not inhibit the change process. There are reasons why middle management is sometimes cruelly referred to as the 'black hole' of management, and one of the major ones has to do with the inability of some managers to 'let go' of information about change. Everyone – regardless of status, rank, or position on the organizational or departmental flow chart – must *understand* what change is taking place, why it is happening, and, most importantly, what the benefits of the change will be. When information is withheld, for whatever reason, a barrier comes up between the withholder of the information and those associated with the change who need it. Keeping information moving throughout the organization and the information services unit which is a part of it, is critical to the success of the change process. In change management, openness is all.

Change is not something we can choose or not choose. As information services managers, regardless of the 'type' of information their units are responsible for, attempt to become part of the power structure of the organization at large, their leadership in the change process is recognized throughout the organization and they become, in both Kanter's and Dalziel and Schoonover's terms, 'heroes' within the organization. They become known as 'information leaders', the people who can guide the organization or community as it seeks to 'keep up' in the ever-expanding information 'explosion'. As such, they put to rest the misperceptions of those who would relegate information services provision to just another 'service' in the organization, and the subservience once associated with the organization, management, and delivery of information services and products is, thankfully, lost forever.

References

Barnard, Chester I. *Organization and Management*. Cambridge, MA: Harvard University Press, 1948.

Bennis, Warren. *On Becoming a Leader*. Reading, MA: Addison-Wesley, 1989.

Drucker, Peter F. *Managing the Nonprofit Organization: Principles and Practices*. New York: HarperCollins, 1990.

Curzon, Susan C. *Managing Change*. New York: Neal-Schuman, 1989.

Dalziel, Murray M. and Schoonover, Stephen C. *Changing Ways: A Practical Tool for Implementing Change Within Organizations*. New York: American Management Association, 1988.

Gardner, John W. *The Nature of Leadership*. Washington, DC: Independent Sector, 1986.

Griffiths, José-Marie, and King, Donald W. *A Manual on the Evaluation of Information Centers and Services*. New York: The American Institute of Aeronautics and Astronautics, 1991.

Kanter, Rosabeth Moss. *The Change Masters: Innovation and Entrepreneurship in the American Corporation*. New York: Simon and Schuster, 1983.

Labovitz, Judy. 'Managing a special library.' *Journal of Library Administration*. 6 (3), Fall, 1985.

Rollwagen, John. 'Washington: news from the front.' *Inc. Magazine*. 16 (1), January, 1994.

Watson, Tom G. 'The librarian as change agent.' *Advances in Library Administration and Organization*. 2, 1983.

Zaleznik, Abraham. 'Managers and leaders: are they different?' *Harvard Business Review*. May–June, 1977.

Chapter Eight

Strategies for justifying information services within the organization

The problem is this: despite their obvious value to the organizations and communities they support (obvious, that is, to the people in those organizations and communities who are stakeholders in the information delivery process), and despite much good will and established good 'feelings' about libraries and other information services units, these units are frequently taken for granted or, at best, given perfunctory acknowledgement for their part in the successful achievement of organizational or community goals. Not that this dismissive treatment is intentional. Indeed, when asked 'What do you think of the corporate library?' or 'Should we do away with the archives section?' or 'Would it be a good idea to contract out MIS activities?' most respondents jump to the fore and rouse themselves to 'defend' the threatened information unit. Alas, almost immediately thereafter they forget about that spirited defense, and when it comes time to discuss resource allocation, service enhancements, an expanded user base and similar subjects which require further commitment from the organization or community to the information services unit, the 'value' of the unit is suddenly diminished.

To be fair, what is described here is a little extreme, but it is not really an atypical scenario. Imagine, for example, the information services department in a small law firm. There is no legal 'library', per se, since the partners keep most of the law books, especially the important legal reference books, in their offices, sharing them about as necessary. An 'information center' is in place, however, for supplying some reference and journal routing services, as needed, and for organizing and processing the materials that arrive through the many loose-leaf services to which the firm subscribes. Additionally, the employee in the 'information center' is responsible for the firm's corporate archives. Current records management is handled in an office across the hall from the 'information center', and the employee there, like the employee in the 'information center', reports to the same supervisor, the firm's office manager.

For a variety of reasons, the law firm's 'information center' is seen only as a support function, and proactive and/or innovative activities on the part of the staff member, or the staff member responsible for records management, would be inappropriate and out of place in this organization. Among the reasons for which these information services units (for they are such, since each of them is involved in the organization, storage, retrieval, and delivery of information) are not treated as a critical or vital component of the organization are these: their staff members are perceived as 'clerical' workers, since the work they do is primarily, from the observations of the firm's other staff, clerical in nature: filing, ordering, routing, shelving, etc. The reporting structure in the organization relegates both employees to a role which is strictly supportive, compounded by the fact that their own supervisor is the person who supervises office and other 'clerical' functions. The 'serious' information work, requiring the use of legal reference materials, online searching, etc. is done in the partners' own offices, using the skills of their own assistants and secretarial staff. So while the organization has, in effect, an 'information center', and while, if asked, each of the partners would willingly and enthusiastically refer to the excellence with which the information workers perform their tasks, there would be no thought of 'professional' expertise for these workers and, in fact, the partners' tone would more than likely convey a hint (and perhaps more) of condescension about the work these employees do. They are taken for granted, their work is perceived as routine, and they are part of the firm's overhead function. This situation, sadly, is typical and demonstrates the usual barriers information workers must overcome if they are to enhance their role, and the role of the services they provide, in their organizations.

The need for enhanced recognition and justification is not, of course, limited to those organizations which support – and are supported by – small information services operations. Every information services manager must from time to time confront organizational antipathy or, even, hostility. Certainly in those organizations in which the information services unit is under threat (whether occasionally or as part of an ongoing situation), interest in and support of the information services operation will dissipate in exact proportion to the level of advocacy that has been established within the organization or community for the unit and the services it provides. The clever information services manager builds into his or her management responsibility a process for establishing that advocacy, and he or she will carefully develop and implement a management plan that 'builds in', so to speak, a process that recognizes the value of advocates and political supporters for the information services unit and its programs.

When there is no such plan in place, or when an information services manager inherits a department in which the concepts of advocacy and political support within the organization have not been previously a part of that unit's operation, it is necessary to change the situation. The task can be a major challenge for the information services staff, and especially for the information services manager, but it is a challenge that can be met. Doing so requires the creation and implementation of specific management strategies designed for this very purpose, and much time and effort must be expended in order to bring about enhanced organizational recognition and support. There are those, of course, who will object to these activities, suggesting that they do not have the luxury of such time and effort, or that (for some reason) such efforts are not part of what they should be doing, or that such efforts might be in some way undignified or otherwise inappropriate for information services managers, but they are wrong. In fact, establishing, implementing, monitoring, reviewing, and when necessary, changing management strategies within the information services unit is as much a managerial responsibility for those who supervise information services units as is the provision of the information services and products for the constituent user base they are chartered to serve. Such strategizing, which will incorporate evaluating, justifying and enhancing the information services unit's role within the organization comes with the territory. It is part of information services management, and ignoring or dismissing these strategizing efforts is done at the information services manager's own peril.

Frequently, the position of the information services unit in the organization structure is pointed out as a way of gaining recognition within an organization, but positioning is not necessarily the solution. Most information services managers and their employees are not positioned (no pun intended) to influence where they and the information services units for which they are responsible, are positioned on an organizational flow chart. Of course they can attempt to re-position their units, and indeed some information services managers have been successful in doing so, but by and large, decisions about the place of a department or subunit of an organization or community within the organizational structure is not the purview of the managers and employees of those departments. So while many authorities in the field are eager to advise that in order to enhance the role of the information services unit within the organization it is necessary to reposition that unit from, say, an administrative department with its overhead connotations to a research and development section with its 'built-in' information values, the advice is short of the mark. Repositioning takes place, if it happens at all, as a *result* of the information products and services provided by the information services unit, not because senior management has been petitioned to do so by the information services staff or because the manager of the information services unit wants it to happen. When the organization has been specifically made aware of the value of its information unit, through the quality of the information products and services provided by that unit, re-positioning will occur if and when senior management decides that such re-positioning is necessary for the overall benefit of all units and staff of the organization or community.

Similarly, concerns about the closing of an information services unit are often predicated on the 'unfairness' or 'thoughtlessness' of organizational or community decision makers, but in fact, by the time a unit has been targeted for closure, it is too late for the information services staff to do anything about the role of the unit in the organization. There are few stories sadder than those of information services managers who find themselves 'surprised' that their units have been so targeted, but in every case, those managers either assumed that they and their units, as information units, were invulnerable to managerial cutbacks or, worse, they conveyed an arrogance about their units and the services the units provided that offended, or at least put off, the decision makers in the organization. Take for example the information services director in one of the regional offices of a large accounting firm. He was known as a man who loved and enjoyed to the envy of others in his field the perquisites of his position, although his unit, which had been created and was managed to provide basic, easy-to-find information for the various employees of the office, was never a 'powerhouse' within the firm. He himself worked behind a closed office door, and his staff, none of whom ever worked for him for more than a couple of years at a time, were trained by him to handle all queries themselves. He was, in fact, director in name only, for he seldom had anything to do with planning or implementing information services for the organization. When the company was merged with another firm, resulting also in the merging of the new company's two information services departments, he of course lost his job, and his unit's efforts were in fact discounted and quickly assimilated into the new information services structure. He had not bothered to put himself forward, he assumed that he was doing a good job because no one ever complained (although his staff heard plenty of complaints, he had trained them to handle difficult problems themselves and not to bother him with them), and his arrogance about the role of information services within the company had left him without a single supporter when it came time to re-organize. Without establishing and implementing strategies for justifying the role of his unit's services within the corporation, he was left flapping in the breeze when the crunch came. It was an ugly picture, but one that could have been much different, if he had only made some effort at putting himself – and his unit – forward within the organization.

Among others, Elizabeth Bole Eddison has established herself as something of an entrepreneurial 'change agent' in this business of working with organizational managements in defining and actualizing the critical role of information services operations within the organization. One of Eddison's great strengths is her ability to advise information services professionals on how to 'sell' management on the value of the information services and products they provide. She has identified such steps as looking at the market for information within the organization, consulting with advisors, defining a financial plan for the services and products to be provided, developing marketing and operations plans, and establishing standards for achieving quality products and services as required, not optional activities in working within an organization for justifying the information services operation. Eddison adheres strongly to a point of view that information services professionals can be the change agents within an organization for providing senior management personnel with an awareness about the value of information and an information services unit for the organization. In fact, as a presenter at a 1991 conference on progress and innovation in the library/ information professional and the role of the librarian/information professional as change agent, Eddison made useful comments about the process, comments which can be valuable to any information services manager with information aspirations higher than the simplest level of information services provision:

> Perhaps being a change agent is part of being a continuum of change. . . . I am a change agent. I know I am. But it wasn't because I sat down and said, I will be a change agent. It's because opportunities keep sliding under the door, or in the window, or over the transom, and if you recognize them and they fit where you are that day, you can march forward. That does make for change. [Information services is] a marvelous profession. It's one of the most creative groups of people I have ever seen. The only limits that we have are because we haven't looked far enough around the next corner. We really can do anything we want. (Eddison, pp. 32–33)

Doing anything we want, of course, includes looking at the services we and our staff provide, using them as a touchstone, as it were, for measuring the value of the information services operation within the organizational structure and, of course, bringing to users, peer groups within the organization, and management the message that, without those services provided by the information services unit and the information services professionals who work there, their own work and the mission of the organization as a whole could not be accomplished.

The political value of information and analysis

Today's information services manager, regardless of the size of the information unit he or she manages or the type of information captured and delivered through the procedures and practices of the unit, is in a catbird seat, as far as his or her strength in the organization is concerned. No one in the organization has as sure a hold on the role of information in the organization, and no one else can work information and analysis to his or her department's advantage as an information services manager can. This advantage has been recognized in the management community at large, and codified by Jeffrey Pfeffer:

> There is little doubt that information, and the certainty that it can provide, is a source of power. It can be used as part of a very important political strategy – getting one's way through analysis. . . . Our belief that there is a right answer

to most situations and that this answer can be uncovered by analysis and illu-
minated with more information, means that those in control of the facts and
the analysis can exercise substantial influence. And facts are seldom so clear
cut, so unambiguous, as we might think. The manipulation and presentation
of facts and analysis are often critical elements of a strategy to exercise power
effectively. . . . (Pfeffer, pp. 247–248)

Despite an apparent desire and intention to use information and analysis
in a rational, straightforward way, as Pfeffer suggests later in his book, that
seldom happens. In fact, much use of information is to support a decision
already made or to put forward a goal or point of view that has already
been chosen. Therefore, for the clever information services manager, the
opportunity to manipulate, organize, and re-package information is always
available, a great boon to the information services manager who wants to
put forward an idea or point of view of his or her own.

Pfeffer has taken this concept of information and analysis as political
tools and addressed the role of the manager within the organization:

There are four useful points to make about information and analysis as political
tactics. First, all organizations strive for the appearance of rationality and the
use of proper procedures, which include using information and analysis to
justify decisions, even if this information and analysis is mustered after the fact
to ratify a decision that has been made for other reasons. In constructing the
appearance of legitimate and sensible decision processes, the use of outside
experts, particularly expensive outside experts, is especially helpful. Such
experts are at once legitimate sources of information and analysis and at the
same time likely to be responsive to the needs of their specific clients within
the organization. Second, in complex, multidimensional decisions such as those
faced by high-level managers, it is very unlikely that processes of straightforward analysis will clearly resolve the issue of what to do. This means that,
third, there is room for the advocacy of criteria and information that favor one's
own position, or, in other words, there is the opportunity to use information
and analysis selectively.

Some might argue that even if information and analysis cannot fully determine
the quality of decisions before they are made, decision quality does become
known after the fact, leading to a process of learning over time. People who
misuse information and analysis for their own political ends, the argument goes,
will eventually be 'uncovered' when decisions or results turn out badly. This
learning will ensure that, over time, better information and better analysis are
rewarded and incorporated into the organization's standard operating
procedures. . . . However, there is little evidence that these assumptions are true,
and there are numerous examples of organizations behaving, for quite
predictable reasons, in exactly the opposite way. The last point, then, is simply
that the discovery of decision quality is both a difficult process and one that is
often assiduously avoided in organizations of all types. As a consequence, the
opportunity to use information and analysis as a potent political weapon is available, and those with the skills and knowledge of how to do so can often gain
substantial power and influence in their organizations. (Pfeffer, pp. 248–249)

For the information services executive and his staff, these four useful points that Pfeffer has identified might be appropriated for the benefit of the information services operation within the parent organization or community. For example, despite the perhaps cynical tone, the staff of the information services unit can play the very same (and perhaps better) role as those 'expensive' outside experts, simply because the information services staff has the ability to obtain, manipulate, analyze, re-package, and deliver the very information that will be used to support the points of view being espoused.

Second, in their role as interpreters, counsellors, and 'navigators' of information, the staff of the information services unit can determine which information is not dealt with in a 'straightforward' manner and add to it the appropriate 'spin' that the information customer is seeking.

Third, by recognizing that users (especially, perhaps, at the senior management level although, it must be recognized, not necessarily) are seeking information that favors a particular position or point of view, the information services staff, as the providers of the information, can take advantage of the opportunity to use information and analysis selectively, within, of course, ethical and moral guidelines established and adhered to within the organization.

Finally, then, the information services executive and her staff will recognize that information and analysis as a 'potent political weapon' can be used to advance the role of the information services operation. It is a role that the information services staff is uniquely skilled to embrace, and when it is used to advance the cause of information services management within the organization, and to demonstrate the value of the information process in the organization's achievement of its goals, the information services operation is, indeed, able to gain that 'substantial power and influence in their organizations' that Pfeffer advocates.

Measuring organizational awareness/raising organizational awareness

The first step toward establishing what might be called a 'justification strategy' is to look at the organizational and/or community structure in order to determine the level of organizational awareness about information services. While this activity takes into consideration the organizational or corporate culture, as described in Chapter Two, it does not relate exclusively to the culture, simply because the focus in any justification or evaluation activity for any department or subunit of the organization will be on that department, and not on the organization's or community's culture as a whole.

One begins by looking at the mission of the information services unit, for if the mission statement has been properly designed, it will state clearly who the information services unit has been created to serve, and it is with this group that the 'awareness' measure can begin. If, for example, the information services unit is located in a manufacturing plant, say, but its mission, as defined at its establishment, is to serve the information needs of a particular subunit or department of the plant, the constituent user group is limited to that subunit or department. The materials testing section, for example, might have its own collection of standards and technical reports and maintain its own contractual agreements for online database services and/or CD-ROM subscriptions, so its constituent user base is fairly well defined. While it is part of the larger organizational picture, its staff and its users are primarily concerned with information related to their particular interests. As part of the larger organization, of course, the unit will respond to enquiries from staff from other sections, but its primary purpose remains one of serving the information needs of the members of the materials testing section.

At the other extreme is the departmental information services unit which becomes, in the absence of a unit specifically chartered to serve the organization as a whole, the *de facto* information unit for the organization. A large utilities company, for example, might boast a very splendid legal library, but in the absence of a corporate library for serving the needs of the executive offices, the manager of the legal library finds herself and her staff doing 'double duty', as it were, working both as a legal library and as a corporate library, a situation which is bound to lead to conflicts and dissatisfaction.

So the first question to ask is, who is the information unit chartered to serve? If the constituent user base is not spelled out in the mission statement, there is probably some 'understanding' about who the users are expected to be, and the information services manager will make some effort to obtain data about how this user base has been determined and whether or not it accurately reflects the needs and interests of the organization at large.

The next step in determining an 'awareness quotient' about information services within the organization is to look at the number of people who make use of the information services unit, in order to determine what percentage of the jurisdiction population they represent. Such information, of course, also reveals what portion of the constituent user base is not served, and the staff of the information services unit can then undertake to determine why these people do not avail themselves of the information services operation and its products and services. Imagine, for example, a small real estate firm in which current records are available through, say, the office of the chief accountant. Once the firm has completed a transaction and all legal and financial requirements have been met, the records of the transaction remain in the accounting office for a year, after which they are sent to the firm's off-site corporate archives facility. The corporate archivist is not particularly concerned that most of the firm's staff do not ever come to her for information, or that her primary 'users', as it were, consist of a group of administrative assistants in various departments who access corporate archives only when seeking information about a transaction sometime in the company's past history. The mission statement for her operation, the corporate archives, makes it clear that hers is a storage or warehouse facility, providing materials when needed but primarily existing so that the company can meet its legal obligations for retaining necessary records of each of its transactions. If she studied the parent organization and its information needs, the fact that organizational awareness is minimal and that most of the firm's staff do not use the archives is not a cause for alarm. The archives do not exist for current, ongoing information service.

On the other hand, an analysis of organizational awareness in the same firm's market research library might reveal a different situation. While a 'core' group of users exists, the library manager and his staff know, from their own general perceptions, that other people in the organization could avail themselves of the services of the market research library with beneficial results. If the market research library was established to serve to research needs of the organization as a whole, and if, for example, of a staff of forty only five or six use the library with any frequency, the staff in the library would be well advised to meet with other staff to determine first, whether they were aware of what the library could provide for them and, second, if they are aware, why they are not using the services of the library.

In this situation, a well-thought out campaign for educating the company's employees about what the market research library offers, and what its services could mean for them in better sales, easier work habits, etc. would result in a definite heightening of awareness about the library. First of all, most people in their normal work patterns simply do not think about libraries and other information services operations. They think of information, rightly so, as a commodity, as nothing more than something to be acquired as and when they need it. Unless they are in some way involved in the library and its operation (as members of a corporate library 'committee', for example, or as part of an organizational funding team that reviews departmental expenditures), most people simply are not 'aware' of libraries and information services units until they require some piece of information that can only be obtained through that information services unit. By going to them and asking these employees about their information needs, many people will be surprised that the library could provide what they need and they will, in fact, begin to make use of the library. Their awareness will have been raised and they will benefit from the information services manager's efforts to make them more knowledgeable about what the market research library is and what it can do for them.

A second useful result of awareness-raising efforts on the part of the information services staff will be the factual demonstration that some of the people in the organization – perhaps a significant percentage of the group – simply have no need for the market research library. Not that having these results is a bad thing, for many employees in any organization have limited need for all types of information, and for many of these, what they need is available in the records and materials they have accessible in their own offices or on their own databases (or corporate databases available in their desktop computers), and they have no further information needs connected with their work. Having this information, and the numbers of staff in this position, is valuable to the information services manager for he can now move ahead with planning information services and products without considering these employees' needs in the planning (unless, of course, his and his staff's research determines that these employees do have information needs that should be addressed in the market research library, but are not – in this case, further effort on his part to determine how the library can meet those needs is required).

At the same time that the information services staff is conducting research about nonusers, a survey of users, in order to determine their awareness of products and services available to them, and their perceived value of the information services unit, should be undertaken. Most of these people will, of course, express satisfaction with the services they receive, but the value of the survey will come from raising their awareness about other products and services that they, for one reason or another, do not realize are available to them. One of the most striking examples turns up in a charitable organization in which the charity's information center is used heavily for staff support (particularly in support of the publicity department, the executive offices, educational programs, and information about the charity's subject field for the general public) but which is relatively unused by the charity's development office, the very people involved in raising money for the organization. Even though the information center's mission specifically states that it exists to support all staff functions as well as external requests for information, for some reason or other, the development staff only used the information center for standard 'library' purposes, with journals routed to them, being on the information center's SDI list, and, when required, borrowing books for office use. Until the staff in the development office was specifically targeted for an awareness-raising campaign, it never occurred to the chief development officer that the information center could be used for procuring information about targeted organizations for funding possibilities, for tracking fund-raising trends, for the development of new donor markets, and the like. Once the development staff was made aware that these and other information 'possibilities' were available to them, the value of the information center increased dramatically in the organization.

Another step for raising awareness has been mentioned before, and it is, in the opinion of many, the wave of the future as far as information services is concerned. Elizabeth Orna, mentioned earlier, is a strong advocate of integrated information within an organization or community, and her criteria for a successful information policy includes a strong integration of external and internal information resources. In the large organization, Orna recommends the development of an organizational information policy for a variety of reasons, and first among these is the fact that when all information activities are integrated, it becomes possible 'to mobilize all sources of information to contribute to the totality of the enterprise's objectives. . . . Because an information policy is developed by bringing together distributed knowledge of all information resources and activities in the enterprise, it is capable of promoting co-operation and openness rather than hostility or concealment among those who are responsible for different aspects of information management,' with the result that these free flows of information point to successful innovation in the transfer of information (Orna, p. 21).

When information flows freely, the source for that information, particularly if it is an established information services unit such as a library, records management department, organizational archives, or a similar operation within the enterprise, the organization as a whole moves forward and the information services unit is recognized for its innovative and encouraging role in that success, a point not lost on Tom Peters in his recipes for success in what he calls the 'nanosecond nineties'. As he lists the elements of the changing nature of organizational relationships, two, in this context, stand out: within the organization, a new appreciation of (and requirement for) trust, which Peters defines simply as 'a willingness to share virtually *everything* with *everybody*', and the creation of electronic (and, it might be suggested, non-electronic as well) information systems 'that can be used across functional boundaries' (Peters, p. 122). Surely the information services unit within an organization or community responsible for developing and managing such innovative and creative information systems will be well regarded within the larger structure.

There is no requirement, however, that considerations about an integrated information system be limited to only the largest organizations. Elizabeth Bole Eddison, whose ideas about the role of change in the management of information services units were discussed earlier in this chapter, also recommends an integration of information resources, through the corporate or organizational library or other information services unit. Eddison refers to this approach as 'raising your visibility' within the organization, and from her point of view, the integration of information resources can play a critical role in raising the awareness of others in the community or organization – users, peers, and management – about the value of the information services unit within the organization. In discussing the value of automated information records within a company, Eddison notes that automated record keeping is brought into an organization for a variety of reasons, including the streamlining of certain processes, setting up an online catalog, simplifying serials and document management and the like.

But many information services managers, Eddison contends, forget about another important benefit, which comes when organizational management agrees to add information about other resources, those not specifically connected with a library, information center, records management department, or other unit that is being put online. And these managers are frequently surprised to discover how much more value their departments have, once they have incorporated information about other organizational operations into their own online system.

'Much information throughout an organization is underused,' says Eddison, 'and that's because there is no easy way for people to find or even know that these resources exist. By adding them to the database in a library or other information services department, that unit adds value.'

Eddison has identified a long list of information resources from various departments outside the information services unit which can be integrated into that unit's database, adding value to the database. Among these are the following, which can provide examples for the managers of any library or information services unit, regardless of size:

From research and development
Internal R&D reports
Product literature
Overhead transparencies
Technical reports
Competitors' technical reports
Conference proceedings
Vendor catalogs
Reprints
External databases
Newsletters
Engineering drawings
Industry standards
Manuals and handbooks
Project files
Test results
Videotapes
Software manuals

From the purchasing office
Vendor catalogs
Distributor information
Supplier files

From the legal department
Export regulations
Case files
Law books
Legal directories
Looseleaf services
Legal periodicals

External databases
Legal memoranda

From corporate offices
Annual reports
Planning magazines
Management publications
Company manuals
Competitors' manuals
Newsletters
Business periodicals
Company or organizational archives
Looseleaf services
Trade publications
Consultants' reports
Audit reports

From computer services
Data tapes
Program tapes
Equipment manuals
User manuals
Supply catalogs
Newsletters
Computer magazines

From the marketing department
Census information
Marketing studies
Consultants' studies
International directories
Advertising campaigns
Competitors' annual reports
Slides of presentations
Videotapes
Tape recordings
Newsletters
Marketing journals
Presentations (Eddison, interview, p. 3)

A third approach toward justifying the value of an information services operation in an organization or community, and in raising the awareness of the constituent user group or groups about the services and products available, is to take a hard look at the information services unit's marketing plan. What works and what does not? Every information services unit has a marketing plan in place. It may or may not be designated as such, but in fact all efforts towards providing information say something about how the unit and its services and products are marketed. According to the experts, there is no question about the value of a marketing plan, and if one is not in place for the library or other information services unit within an organization or community, the services and programs that the department provides will not be as effective as they could be. Arlene Farber Sirkin defines the marketing plan as 'a formal process through which the organization can fulfill its mission' and suggests that the process of developing a marketing plan 'provides a structure for the organization to identify the user groups that the organization, within the context of its mission, seeks to serve and to identify their needs'. Using the plan, Sirkin suggests, enables the organization to identify, establish, promote, and evaluate a group of services and products aimed at satisfying those needs. The plan, according to Sirkin, 'provides a tool to focus limited staff, time, and money for maximum effectiveness' (Sirkin, p. 1).

Bettiann Welch, a trainer in the marketing field, contends that four out of five enterprises fail because they do not have a marketing plan, and she offers six steps - which can be applied to the information services field - for formulating such a plan:

1. *Diagnosis*. Where are you going, and why?

2. *Prognosis*. Where are you headed if you continue on this path?

3. *Goals and objectives*. Plan at least one year ahead by asking yourself: What new markets do I want to develop?

4. *Strategy*. How are you going to get there?

5. *Tactics*. Draw yourself a road map. Who will do what, and when?

6. *Control*. How are we doing? (Welch, p. 57)

It is, of course, this last question that determines how well, or not, the information services unit's programs are working. By asking hard questions about who is using the information service unit's products and services and how that use affects the work that they do within the organization or community, the manager of the unit is not only raising awareness about the value of the unit within the larger enterprise, but acquiring information that he or she can use for developing better and more responsive services and products for the users.

Organizational evaluations

The specialized library, information center, records management department or other information services unit is but one part of a larger enterprise, and only those information services managers who understand that fact and incorporate it into their department's operation will be able to function successfully within the larger organization or community. Too often, information professionals see themselves and their units as a 'stand-alone' operation, a fact which accounts for much wasted effort and misunderstanding within the information services field. The smart information services managers recognizes that the information services for which he or she is responsible is 'judged', to use Herbert S. White's word, against overall organizational goals and objectives. Whether or not that unit will be able to grow and improve will depend upon how the unit matches up to those overall goals and objectives. The unit's contribution to those goals must be claimed, White correctly asserts, and while this claim might be difficult to prove, it is not difficult to 'demonstrate as reasonable'. White continues, offering useful guidelines for the information services manager:

> Here we must distinguish among three terms frequently used in organizational evaluations – efficiency, effectiveness and cost benefit. Efficiency . . . means simply that whatever is being done is accomplished as quickly and cheaply as possible, whether or not the tasks are the 'right' ones.
>
> Effectiveness demonstrates the *value* of what is being done. The special library's [or other information services unit's] value is in providing service to its users. . . . (White, p. 99)

Cost benefit is defined by White as 'the "proven" reduction in other costs or the increase in income because of the effective presence of the special library'.

Some management authorities in the information services field, including White, suggest that cost benefit, for an information service unit, is difficult if not impossible to demonstrate, but in fact studies have been done in which the value of the information services operation can be quantified. For example, Joanne G. Marshall's study, in 1991 and early 1992, addressed this issue. Marshall asked executives in the corporate environment how a specific information services unit (in this case the organization's special library) impacted upon decision making in the corporation. Not only was she able to prove that information provided by the library often contributed toward the ability of managers and executives to exploit new business opportunities (63.9 percent of the respondents), over half of these managers and executives reported that the information had enabled them to approve a financial transaction. Reversing the process, 47.8 percent of the respondents indicated that an actual loss of funds was prevented because of information supplied by the special library, and some 40 percent of these organizations avoided the loss of a client because the information supplied by the special library indicated that the loss could be prevented (Marshall, pp. 19–22). These and similar conclusions must be pointed out to senior management on an ongoing basis, in order to emphasize and reinforce, to those decision makers within the organization, the value of the information services unit.

Challenging organizational perceptions

If recognizing the value of (and acting upon) organizational evaluation procedures is part of the process for developing strategies for justifying and evaluating information services, equally important is the opportunity presented by the organizational structure to challenge how libraries and other information services units are perceived within the organization or community they have been created to support. There is, as has been described, a need to assess the organizational or institutional culture, in order to match the culture of the information services unit to that of the organization itself.

A second approach is to engage in an exercise of self-analysis. All employees of the information services unit might want to participate in this activity, but certainly the manager of the unit and his or her immediate associates should look at themselves from the perspective of those who are using the information services and products provided by the department, other peers within the organization (whether they are clients or not), and of course management personnel to whom they report. Addressing librarians in this context, F. Woody Horton offered good advice which, with appropriate adaptations, can be applied to almost every information services worker:

> [An] area that has been well documented in the literature is the problem of the librarian's image. To put it simply: If you see yourself as a librarian or an individual in the workplace whose primary task is to acquire, catalog and manage books and other traditional library materials, then others will see you as a librarian. We have been conditioned to identify librarians by the work they do, by attitude, by behavior, and so on. That's fine if you wish to remain working as a librarian in a traditional library setting.
>
> Most librarians see themselves as outstanding organizers and controllers of physical library holdings. And they are! Librarians are experts at identifying, describing, measuring, retrieving, distributing and controlling books, serials and non-print media. Acquisitioning, cataloging, indexing, abstracting and similar functions are the lifeblood of librarianship as it is taught in most library schools today.
>
> But if you see yourself, on the other hand, as an individual who helps others identify their information needs, then find and seek out that needed information, accessing it efficiently, obtaining delivery in a cost-effective manner, and then effectively utilizing the information, then you will be seen more as an information professional in the broader sense, than as a librarian in the narrower, traditional sense. You may, first and foremost, be a librarian, but because of unfortunate stereotypes, others may see you in a different light. (Horton, p. 13)

It is, of course, up to each information services manager to establish a milieu in which they themselves and their employees can engage in actions for changing perceptions about what they do. Since so much effort has been concentrated within the information services field on the 'image' of the information worker, numerous guidelines exist, but the best 'test', so to speak, for an information services manager is to impart to his or her staff the value of looking at the services and products they provide through the eyes of the user, the layperson who is not sophisticated in the study of information services as a separate field of scientific endeavor, and who, in any case, could not care less about such matters. If the information staff (in any organization or community, and dealing with any form of information services) can see themselves and their work as their clients see them, the stage is set for changing perceptions about what information workers do. This point was best made in a paper delivered by Ann W. Talcott at a conference in November 1993. Entitled 'Indispensable or Expendable? Making Yourself Valuable to Your Organization', Talcott's paper offered a number of helpful directions for information services managers, and in terms of looking at the information services operation from the customer's viewpoint, she listed five essential questions to be asked:

1. What are my service standards? Do they meet my customers' expectations?

2. How does the physical layout of the library [or other information services unit] impact information service?

3. Are rewards for 'service-mindedness' built into my staff's performance review?

4. How many repeat customers do staff members have?

5. Do I review my staff's attitude and behavior toward customers? (Talcott, p. 6)

Similar introspective behavior might be applied by the information services manager to an analysis of the organization itself, an exercise probably already undertaken as the organizational or institutional culture was studied. Nevertheless, in this context, some considerations might be in order, as the information services manager attempts to link the work that he or she is doing with that of the organization. Primarily, what one is seeking here is a match between the 'type' of organization of which the information services unit is a part, and the 'type' of department in which the information services staff works. Think about, for example, a public relations firm in which the corporate information center exists primarily to track industry trends, to identify prospective clients, and to provide supporting documentation for the firm's account managers when they are engaged in projects with clients. The organizational 'type' is one of fast-paced, high-end information turnaround, and the information center will be expected to match the organization's 'tone' in the information services and products it provides. In fact, if it does not, if there is a mismatch between the 'tone' of the organization and the 'tone' of the information center, it is only a matter of time before the mismatch (perceived as a lack of sympathy to one another's efforts by each party) will result in a dissolution of the information center or, hopefully, a radical restructuring.

A useful perspective from which to look at the 'match' or 'balance' between an organization and its information services operation is the level of teamwork between the manager of the information services unit and senior management within the organization. If, for example, the organizational structure places the information services unit, a records management department, say, under the jurisdiction of a vice-president for administrative services, and that senior management employee is not interested in or available for consultations about departmental policies and programs, the level of teamwork between the manager of the records management unit and the person she reports to will be a negative one and will, more than likely, adversely affect the ability of the records manager to plan proactive records management services for the employees and other information customers who need to access the information captured in the section. On the other hand, an interested senior management employee, one who actively encourages innovation, high customer services standards, and proactive information delivery practices within the records management department, and who is open and available for consultations about organizational matters with the manager of the department, will have established an ambiance within the organization that leads to a high level of excellence in the delivery of information from the department. The level of teamwork is high between the two managers, and each of them recognizes that the other is a valuable partner in the achievement of the organization's mission, whatever that might be.

Assessing information delivery

For all information services operations, information values within the organization or community being served contribute to a major strategy in justifying and evaluating the success of the information delivery unit. While these values may vary somewhat in intensity or emphasis, depending on the host organization (and the organizational culture) of which the unit is a part, they can generally be summed up in a set of agreed-upon standards that most information services departments observe. For information customers and those senior management personnel to whom information services managers report, accuracy, timeliness, high use value, low cost, and information services better than those provided by competing information providers are the criteria upon which information services units are judged.

Accuracy, for example, generally heads the list of any information customer's needs. When he or she comes into an information services unit to have a problem solved, nothing dissipates his or her goodwill further than to be forced to re-do the search because the information provided was 'wrong' information. In many cases, the request is so specific that no error is possible: in a hospital's patient records section, for example, bringing up the records for Patient A when the request was for Patient B is a useless and wasteful procedure. The requester of the information for a particular patient has no use for someone else's records.

At the other extreme, however, are those situations where the judgement of the information provider comes into play, and the accuracy of the information is subject to interpretation. Unless the information customer has specifically asked for a history of a particular subject, the information services provider offering him a chronological range of corporate archives when he is specifically seeking an advertising campaign used in 1958 will be of little value. On the other hand, if he is seeking information about the company's advertising activities during the decade of the fifties, such a range of material will be useful.

Timeliness, too, affects the delivery of an information product, and customers determine the worth of a service often on the basis of the timeliness of a piece of information. If an author needs a fact checked in a hurry and calls a magazine's editorial library and conveys her query into a voice-mail system, or leaves an e-mail message, she expects a return message as soon as possible. If the message is not returned by the time she must finish the article she is working on, the query process is useless to her and she must use another method for checking that fact.

Similarly, high use value affects organizational perceptions about the value of an information service, a problem that affects many who are responsible for corporate or organizational archives facilities. In an effort to reduce overhead and the use of hard copy documents, a major research organization with a century-long history of providing grants for scientific expeditions decided to retain only the grant records and the final report of the expedition. All other documentation was deemed unnecessary, and while electronic versions of the grant records and final reports were preferred by the management team responsible for implementing the new 'paperless' record system, the influence of older staff was brought to bear on senior management and, grudgingly, a single paper copy of the final report was also retained. Unfortunately, all other documentation relating to the expeditions, including correspondence from the various scientists who travelled on the expeditions, as well as correspondence among the different scientists, was not retained, and after less than ten years the organization's modern archives, as archives, were useless to most of the user group which had been accessing them in the past. Before the decision had been made to retain only minimal materials, no studies among the users had been done, resulting in minimal use value for them, of the materials that were available.

Low cost, of course, continues to be a primary evaluative tool for judging the value of an information services unit and, from a management point of view, is often invoked as a reason for closing down or otherwise dispensing with an information section in an organization. If management can be made to accept that a cheaper method exists for supplying the information that the unit is providing, it will seek that cheaper method. Similarly, the information provided by an information services unit must be better than whatever competition for those information services exists elsewhere, or a decision will be made to go to the competition. A useful example occurred in an agency of the US Federal Government. Chartered by the US Congress to review certain technical developments in a field of environmental concern, this agency had hired a librarian to put together a collection of technical reports and journals when, in fact, each of the members of the review team was affiliated with an academic or research institution where the materials were already available. In each case, the team members went first to their own scientific collections for the materials they needed and only when, for one reason or another, the materials were not available, did they contact the agency's 'library'. Needless to say, after a very short time, the agency's collection fell into a state of desuetude, the role of the manager of the unit was minimized and the position eventually eliminated. The 'library', as a library, was disbanded, for it had been an expensive and unnecessary 'experiment' in creating a library where none was needed. The competition for the services the unit was to provide was too great, and there was no way the agency's collection, located at a remove from even the nearest geographic team member, could match the team member's own institution for convenience, to say nothing of the cost of delivering the materials.

Quality service

In the final analysis, of course, the single viable criterion for the justification and evaluation of an information services operation is the quality of the information products and services it provides to its constituent user group. Much attention is given today to quality service standards, and while some leaders in other disciplines would appear to regard total quality management, quality 'circles', quality assurance, and similar approaches to the subject as passé and without merit, in fact, particularly in information services, the concepts of total quality management are critical to the successful delivery of the products and services that information customers have a right to expect. Anne M. Fredenburg has even suggested that for information services units that are on an unsure footing with senior management, 'establishing a quality assurance program may provide the key' for strengthening a relationship with management (Fredenburg, p. 277).

Quality assurance is variously defined in the literature, and for information services management, the concepts identified in Michael Barrier's paper on total quality management in 1992 are most appropriate (and frequently referred to by this author):

Fortunately, there is no real mystery about TQM. After more than a decade of quality programs, there is wide agreement on their essential ingredients. Among them:

An intense focus on customer satisfaction   'The essence of TQM is that you should be customer-driven', says Richard L. Lesher, president of the US Chamber of Commerce, which recently announced plans for a TQM program. TQM's definition of 'customer' embraces internal as well as external customers. An employee in the shipping department may be the internal 'customer' of an employee who completes assembly of a product, just as the person who buys that product is the customer of everyone in the company.

Accurate measurement   Using a fistful of readily available statistical techniques, of every critical variable in a business's operations. TQM companies use those measurements to trace problems to their roots and eliminate their causes.

Continuous improvement of products and services   TQM is not a static concept; by eliminating chronic problems, it opens the way to never-ending innovation.

New work relationships based on trust and teamwork   Central to TQM is empowerment, through which management gives employees wide latitude in how they go about achieving the company's goals. (Barrier, pp. 22–23)

To Barrier's concepts must be added another: the total and enthusiastic commitment of management at all levels within the organization. While information services managers can, and do, embrace quality assurance programs for their units, the success of those programs is directly related to the level of enthusiasm and commitment of the senior management to whom they report.

This leads, usefully, to a definition for quality assurance in information services, as provided by Fredenburg. Quality assurance, she writes, is 'a systematic method of establishing standards, identifying and monitoring problems, and looking for ways to improve where improvement is possible' (Fredenburg, pp. 277–278). Information services managers, therefore, in moving towards quality services will put into place methods and procedures that will enable them to identify and act upon their information customers' needs, while, at the same time, looking for every opportunity for innovation and improving the methods and procedures that have already been established. Among the techniques that they will employ are the following:

Planning

No information services manager is so busy that he or she cannot find the time to plan, for planning is an essential component in delivering information services and products that meet the needs of the established user base.

If the other tasks of managing the department interfere with one's planning abilities, an objective, no-nonsense look at how one spends one's time, including an equally tough look at how and when one says 'no' to certain requests, will be beneficial.

Aggressive/proactive management

To know what customers want and need from an information services unit, the manager of that unit will get out of the office and move around amongst the staff of the organization, learning what projects people are working on and how they determine their information needs. Combining this data with a planning model designed to meet information needs will establish the information services operation as a major player in the achievement of the organization's or community's goals.

Continuous improvement

As a specific component of the quality management philosophy, information services managers and their staff will be constantly on guard for dissatisfaction among customers and will actively seek to create innovative policies and procedures for removing the causes of those dissatisfactions.

Problem-solving

Information customers come to an information services unit for one reason only: to address a problem that can be resolved by acquiring the correct information. If the solution to the specific problem is within the purview of the information services unit's defined mission, when the problem is not solved, the information services department has failed. No amount of posturing or excusing will change that basic fact.

Evaluation

Measuring the quality of the services and products emanating from the information services unit, regardless of the kind of information unit it is, requires several basic steps that must be incorporated into the management system that is followed in the department. Among these are the following:

Brief, written survey questionnaire On a regular basis, customers of an information services unit must be asked if their information needs are being met. The questionnaire does not need to be elaborate (in fact, the simpler the better), but it must address the specific issues the staff of the information unit needs to know (as mentioned above): accuracy, timeliness, high use value, low cost, and competitive information resources.

Survey users by telephone A weekly half-hour on the telephone, discussing the 'success rate' of the information services operation with randomly selected users, will yield a great wealth of usable anecdotal data about the effectiveness of the unit.

Get feedback from former users   On an occasional basis, information services staff should look through activity logs for the names of people who used the products and services of the unit six, nine, and twelve months ago. Why they are not currently using the department should be known.

Put information about service quality to work   When users are surveyed, the information services staff needs to determine how their usage of the information unit affected their work, and effectiveness measures, whenever possible, should be employed. Broadcasting this information within the parent organization can be a useful activity in establishing and promulgating the value of the information services unit throughout the organization.

Keep asking and improving   The information services manager who is serious about his or her work will not be satisfied only with feedback. Every response will elicit the same reaction: 'Could we have done it better?'. Only when an attitude of constant improvement is in place can the information services department, regardless of the information being managed within that department, be secure of its place within the organization.

Addressing issues of quality service leads to a final strategy for today's information services manager who wants to successfully justify and evaluate information services within the organization, and it is a two-fold one. It has been identified and expounded upon by Meg Paul, a leader in the Australian information services field, who has bravely taken it upon herself to express some of the sentiments that have been studiously avoided within the profession. One of these 'avoided' ideas expressly states that the information providers themselves are not exactly innocent of blame as managers and decision makers dismiss and disband libraries, records management units, archives, and other information services units that had once been created to meet critical information needs in their communities and organizations.

At the 1993 Annual Conference of the Australian Library and Information Association, Paul spoke bluntly about the subject. Speaking about special libraries, she stated that 'some of the closures [of special libraries] are the fault of the library staff'. Asking what she called the $64 question, Paul put this to her audience: 'Why have special libraries closed or downsized in these days of information overload, when it appears logical to us that a professional librarian is the person in an organization with the particular attributes, skills and training to sift through the information mass, extract what is important, package it and deliver it to the appropriate person? Why are these libraries closing, especially when the information sector is the sector of largest growth in the Australian economy?' (Paul, 1993, pp. 147–155).

Paul answered the question herself: the reasons can be found in the qualifications and training of the managers to whom special librarians and other information providers report, managers who are generalists, who do not know what a library does, and who see it as an easy item to cut. 'The library,' she said in her presentation, 'is seen as an overhead'. And information professionals are not seen as gatherers and disseminators of information simply because they have been working so hard 'delivering the service' that they have not educated advocates to speak on their behalf and have not been political enough within their own organizations.

In her presentation, Paul continued with her theme, addressing one of the major components of quality management: 'we have not been involved in listening and observing the information needs of our clients. We've been giving them what we think they need, not what they know they need.'

In her pleas for increased attention to the real needs of information customers, Paul looks to the information services staff as a foundation: 'An important part in motivating staff,' she says, 'is appropriate training, recognition of a job well done, and delegation of responsibility with designated areas of responsibility'.

What is needed in every information services operation, according to Paul, is 'a quality service ethos' established and owned by the staff with management support and approval. 'Staff must understand how quality service benefits them with more fulfilling employment, better interpersonal relations, and the approbation and approval of others within the organization.'

According to Meg Paul, survival is also part of the picture. 'If a library does not meet the needs of its clients,' she says, 'the value and integrity of the information it provides is not recognized, and the library is not able to prove its cost effectiveness'. When this happens, 'the library will cease to exist as clients withdraw their support. The clients are the stakeholders and those librarians who do not heed their needs and listen to them will face extinction or radical upheaval.'

It is a frightening prospect, but there is, according to Paul, a way for preventing this radical upheaval: 'In times of restricted budgets and staffing, it is not always possible for a library to deliver all it could deliver,' she said. 'The library must take budget cuts along with other departments. However, due recognition that the library is doing all it can under existing circumstances is very important to communicate. *An astute librarian should realize that an excellent service still needs advocates within the organization.* . . . There are always occasions when you will need advocates to lend support in internal political situations and these will usually be clients who value your services.'

These clients Meg Paul identifies as the information services unit's 'insurance policy'. The service must be sold to the clients, Paul contends, 'but you cannot sell an effective service unless you are delivering one. If libraries are to survive tough economic times, they must have a fully paid up insurance policy, an educated and satisfied clientele who know that you and your library provide an excellent service, who will support the library. These are the users who understand the value of the information you supply. And they also understand the value of what you do. For this alone they must be cultivated.'

In 1991, writing in the *Australian Library Journal*, Paul published what has become something of a 'service manifesto' for information services professionals, and her list is striking for two demands which, in her opinion, are not negotiable: first, that information services professionals, as professionals, are always *pleased* with the work they do, but never *satisfied*. 'We know that no search we do, either online or manual, can be perfect. A vital link may have been missed, and as we cannot be experts in all subjects we may not recognize this. So we're constantly striving to provide better information, to deliver a better information product.' (Paul, 1991, p. 65).

Paul's second major assertion is one that most information services professionals avoid like the plague: 'The client is always right'. For many information professionals, who see their role as one of educating, arbitrating, setting the standards and so forth, 'giving in' to the client is an admission of some sort of failure, some lack of success.

Not so, according to Paul. 'When we say the client is always right, even when wrong, what we mean is simply that I, as an information deliverer, cannot afford to offend or humiliate any client in any way. The client may with malice or without malice make a remark which could affect the library and staff adversely. Even when the client has realized that he or she is wrong, that person will appreciate not being confronted with it. After all, lawyers, accountants and doctors have fragile egos, and engineers and scientists, while a little more reasonable, don't want to be confronted either. An intelligent member of staff can always present the information requested, together with the information their professional judgement has deemed to be required, in such a way that the inquirer will not lose face. And when that happens, the library has acquired a new advocate.'

References

Barrier, Michael. 'Small firms put quality first.' *Nation's Business*. 80 (5), May, 1992.

Eddison, Elizabeth Bole. 'The entrepreneur as change agent: innovation through product and service genesis.' *Agents of Change: Progress and Innovation in the Library/Information Profession*, edited by Jana Varlejs. Jefferson, NC: McFarland and Company, 1992.

Eddison, Elizabeth Bole. Interview with the author. February 22, 1994.

Fredenburg, Anne M. 'Quality assurance: establishing a program for special libraries.' *Special Libraries*. 79 (4), Fall, 1988.

Horton, Forest Woody. *Extending the Librarian's Domain: A Survey of Emerging Occupation Opportunities for Librarians and Information Professionals*. Washington, DC: Special Libraries Association, 1994.

Marshall, Joanne G. *The Impact of the Special Library on Corporate Decision-Making*. Washington, DC: Special Libraries Association, 1993.

Orna, Elizabeth. *Practical Information Policies: How to Manage Information Flow in Organizations*. Aldershot, England: Gower, 1990.

Paul, Meg. 'Improving service provision.' *The Australian Library Journal.* 22 (10), November, 1991.

Paul, Meg. 'Why special libraries close: a consultant's view.' *Australian Special Library News.* 26 (4), December, 1993.

Peters, Tom. *Liberation Management: Necessary Disorganization for the Nanosecond Nineties*. New York: Knopf, 1992.

Pfeffer, Jeffrey. *Managing with Power: Politics and Influence in Organizations*. Boston, MA: The Harvard Business School Press, 1994.

Sirkin, Arlene Farber. 'Marketing planning for maximum effectiveness.' *Special Libraries.* 82 (1), Winter, 1991.

Talcott, Ann W. 'Indispensable or expendable? Making yourself valuable to your organization.' Unpublished paper presented at the Special Libraries Association Northeast Regional Conference, Rye, NY, November 3, 1993.

Welch, Bettiann. 'Marketing: winning customers with a "workable" Plan.' *Success Magazine*. June, 1990.

White, Herbert S. *Managing the Special Library: Strategies for Success Within the Larger Organization*. White Plains, NY: Knowledge Industry Publications, 1984.

Chapter Nine

The management partnership

Those who would offer superior information products and services discover that their success depends on influence, their own and that of the people within their service sphere who have agreed – tacitly or otherwise – to be their political advocates. The process of acquiring that influence is a subtle and sometimes rather delicate activity, for it is based upon and builds upon certain recognized human traits that all workers bring to and encounter in the workplace, whether they are in the information field or not. Such attributes as personal demeanor, the desire for approval, the desire to serve, ambition, the need for social intercourse, an interest in contributing to the common good, and, most important, the very human need to feel wanted or to be a participant in a successful and valued enterprise, all influence one's movement toward success in one's work.

When these attributes are applied to the delivery of information within an organizational or community structure, one in which the value (however minimal) of the information function has been established and is recognized as a viable component of the enterprise, the role of influence and political advocacy can be appreciated. An information services operation, regardless of its quality or its contribution to the achievement of the organizational mission, is perceived as a stand-alone operation within the organization, community, or enterprise, but this perception must be changed. No matter how good the provision of information services and products, without recognition from beyond the information services unit itself, its influence is minimal and limited to one-on-one interactions between each individual information user and the individual or group within the information services unit which provides the information. The successful information services manager will engage in a number of activities designed to convey to all others in the organization or community that the information services operation is, in fact, an integral component in the achievement of the organization's or community's own success.

Such perceptions within the organization, that is, success as defined in organizational terms, require the wholehearted support of political advocates who not only recognize themselves the value of the information services unit and its contribution to the success of their endeavors, but who are willing to pronounce that success to others, particularly to others with their own influence within the organization or community. The road to recognition within the organization, it seems clear, requires the establishment and ongoing development of a partnership arrangement between the information stakeholders, whether they are users, providers, or decision makers within the organization or community.

In all cases, the analysis begins with an understanding of the role of the information services manager, the basic rudiments of working with senior management within the organization or community, the place of supportive users and peers in the advocacy process, the value of participation in project and team management scenarios, and an understanding of how power is used – and accounted for – in the strategic planning process. In the final analysis, empowerment, influence, and the advocacy of trusted colleagues (at the same level and at levels above and below that of the information services manager within the organizational or community hierarchy) are the groundwork upon which successful information services programs are built. Those information services managers who recognize this state of affairs succeed. Those who do not cannot expect to succeed, no matter how sincere their efforts.

Role of the information services manager

For those who are authorized to provide information services and products in any organization or community, there are several responsibilities which define their work. Ellis Mount, for example, identified specific responsibilities for the information services manager (described in Chapter Six), and for most people involved in information services, Mount's 'relating to top management' and 'evaluating operations' seem to be the best mechanism for changing perceptions (within the organization or community) and for obtaining the support of senior management. In purely practical terms, the two are, in fact, one and the same, for by establishing workable procedures for evaluating operations, the information services manager takes upon himself or herself a management role defined in terms related to organizational or community management.

Take, for example, a scientific research organization in which a technical librarian is employed to organize and retrieve not only technical reports obtained from external sources, but also to organize and retrieve, on demand, the research reports generated internally. Regardless of format or the 'finished' nature of these internal documents, once they have been acquired by the technical library, it is that department manager's responsibility to see that they are available for the research staff as they are needed. Thus the technical librarian must enter into a working relationship – a partnership, if you will – with the organization's research director, so that he or she will know what work is being done in the organization, know what work is being emphasized (as well as what work is temporarily or otherwise relegated to 'the back burner') and what material is likely to be called for as the work progresses.

To achieve this goal, the technical librarian will, of course, engage in the other pursuits Mount has listed, including planning for the appropriate storage and classification procedures, budgeting both time and resources for this effort, organizing his or her staff and the operations of the technical library to meet this goal, and, as the library's collection cannot be utilized until the research organization's staff knows what is there, marketing the collection to the constituent user base. All of these activities are, of course, internal operations within the technical library and of little use or concern to those to whom the manager of the library – the technical librarian – reports. Nevertheless, having entered into this 'partnership' with his or her managers, the technical librarian has an obligation to evaluate the work being done in the library and to convey that evaluation to his or her managers, thus strengthening the relationship between them.

It is here, though, that the technical librarian and the library staff must avoid typical 'library-'type measures, and engage in measurement procedures that senior management will appreciate. For example, while some statistics regarding collection size, volume of use, and similar quantifiable data are of value, the information services manager must also provide information that relates to the point of view that senior management might have about the organization and its success, especially if the information services manager is attempting to enhance the influence of information services within the organization or community.

If, in the example described here, senior management is concerned about staff productivity in other departments, the information services manager should establish a process for tracing, say, the turnaround time in the delivery of information products from the technical library. Not only would monthly comparisons be reported to management, the tracking records might be published in the company's house organ or posted on a bulletin board in a high-visibility area so that all employees in the organization would see what the information services staff is capable of and how it meets or exceeds its own standards. Similarly, if the organization is one in which various departments are publicly recognized for their efforts in the successful achievement of some organizational goal – the awarding of an important contract, perhaps, or the successful roll out of a new product or a component of a new product – the information services unit's role in such success can likewise be acknowledged by the manager of the department and reported to all information stakeholders in the organization, regardless of whether their specific work relates to that activity or not.

What is being established here is a recognition, within the organization or community, that the information services operation plays an important role in the success of that organization or community, and the key to that recognition lies in what Phillip W. Morton identified as the communication process. Writing about the electronic library and the role of the person who manages it, Morton noted as early as 1982 that the information services unit can play a critical role in the organization's overall success:

> I refer to knowledge and information separately, although I believe they are part of the same decision making continuum. It is the function of today's information manager to serve as the catalyst for the change information undergoes on the way to becoming knowledge. And knowledge or the lack of it is the vital ingredient in sound decision making. The all-too-often missing link between the two is communication. Information without communication is about as useful as one chopstick. Therefore, those responsible for information's acquisition, treatment, storage, retrieval, *and* communication become crucial to the successful decision making process within their respective organizations. (Morton, p. 75)

If we can agree that in all cases the 'function' of today's information manager is to serve as a 'catalyst', that manager is behaving foolishly indeed if he or she does not take advantage of the opportunity the information staff has for ensuring that recognition is given to the information services operation not only for delivering the information but for *changing that information into knowledge* as well.

Think about a community of scholars whose organization exists to provide financial support, staff, and information resources to enable the scholars to carry out research about population growth in developing countries. Because the organization is well known, large quantities of unsolicited materials are sent to its staff, and the manager of the information services operation has responsibility for not only distributing the materials to appropriate researchers, but for disposing of unwanted materials. To avoid large backlogs of unread materials in each scholar's office, the information services staff has organized a two-fold approach to the matter. By hiring a literature specialist in population studies as a staff member for the information services department, all unsolicited materials are now reviewed by the literature specialist. Selected materials are abstracted, with the abstracts routed to the scholars in the organization. If they need to see the materials, or if they wish to recommend the abstracted item for addition to the permanent collection, they respond within a particular timeframe. For abstracted materials not selected by the scholars, and for items not chosen for abstracting, a special storage space is set aside, with each item dated when it is added to that 'temporary' collection. Staff and scholars can review the collection at any time, but if items are not reviewed and their status changed within a second established timeframe, the materials are discarded (or given to a scholar for his or her personal collection, if that choice has been requested). In all cases, the scholars have not one but several opportunities to consider the value of unsolicited materials, and the information services staff is able not only to assist the scholars by participating in the process in which information is changed into knowledge, but a procedure has been established which cuts through much of the labor-intensive selection process that is based less on subject knowledge than on a desire to 'move things along'.

This approach to information services management fits conveniently (and appropriately) into a view of information delivery that has been given much attention during the last two decades or so. It was first identified by Shirley Echelman in 1974, when she posited that the information services manager's first responsibility is to work with other information stakeholders and decision-makers in the organization or community, to determine what their needs are. Then, and only then, Echelman declared, is the information services manager in a position to manage the operations of the library (Echelman, pp. 409–410). The order of the effort is important to the discussion of advocacy for an information services unit, for if the information stakeholders in an organization or community are *asked* what their information needs are, their perceptions about their *own* role in the information delivery process automatically becomes one of support. If the information services manager, on the other hand, thinks of the information unit as a stand-alone operation, to be managed according to separate management principles that may or may not relate to the achievement of an organizational or community mission, perceptions within the organization or community about the value of the information services unit are necessarily weakened.

The effort, then, must concentrate on integrating the information services unit into the organization or community as a whole. There are specific techniques for achieving this happy state of affairs, and the list begins with the attitude of the information services manager and the staff who work with him or her in providing the information for the constituent user base. While the subject of his or her work must obviously be 'information' and the delivery of 'information' products and services to the users, the information manager must never be so inured in his or her own professional standing that the service concept – and especially service as it is connected to the achievement of organizational or community goals – is lost. Several authorities have commented that of all the qualities that relate to success in information services management, perhaps the one that is most specific to their work and best characterizes those who are successful is that information managers see themselves as employees *first*, as employees of the organization or community that provides support for their information services units, and then only secondly as members of whatever information services field they are affiliated with (e.g. specialized librarianship, records management, archives management, etc.). In this connection, Ferguson and Mobley (p. 4, pp. 96–97ff.) provide particularly useful guidance.

A similar but not necessarily identical pattern has been identified by James Matarazzo in his studies of specialized libraries and corporate information centers that have been closed or seriously downsized. In these situations, the librarians' perceptions of themselves had to do with their roles as *librarians*, not as *managers*, and it is this distinction which led to their not being 'taken seriously' by organizational management. In fact, it is in learning to think more like managers that librarians and other information services professionals will achieve their success in the organizations and communities in which they work, an idea recognized by John Kok several years ago:

> It has often been said that if special librarians are to survive in the widely heralded information age, they must stop thinking like librarians and start thinking like managers. In fact, a whole new breed of people has sprung up who call themselves 'information managers'. They differ from special librarians not so much in technical know-how as in attitude. They view information in managerial terms: as a resource that has an integral and quantifiable role in helping the organization achieve its operational goals. (Kok, p. 527)

The indispensability factor

In terms of advocacy, political sponsorship, or simply for acceptance into the power structure of the organization or community in which an information services professional is employed, it is critical that one's personal perceptions match – or at least recognize and give credence to – those of other decision makers in the enterprise.

Maintaining such an attitude about one's professional role, and particularly one's place within the organization or community, leads neatly into another subject that relates to information services management, and that is the value of an ongoing, working relationship with senior management and other organizational power brokers as information customers. Ann Talcott, addressing special librarians, raises very basic questions about who information services professionals should market their services to, for it is her strong contention that information workers are perceived as valuable in their organizations in direct proportion to their 'indispensability or expendability' to senior management and others in the organization or community who have power.

Among Talcott's 'commandments' for distinguishing between the indispensability or expendability of an information services unit includes one that is basic to our discussion of advocacy for the unit: 'Thou shalt know thy executives'. Talcott writes:

> While our survival depends upon the creation of demand, we can't be all things to all people. Resources are too limited. So whom will we serve? I suggest that you learn as much as possible about the people who hold the power in your company. In a for-profit organization, identify the people and the departments who bring the money in. In a not-for-profit institution, identify the people who decide how it will be spent. These people are your priority customers.

> We are in a position to assist these decision makers, but they are rarely avid library users. Identify the ones who use your services and those who don't. You can't ignore either group, but your tactics for influencing them will be different. (Talcott, pp. 2–3)

Using Talcott's guidelines, we might reflect on the information services operation in a large advertising agency, for example. Definitely a profit-making organization (or purporting to be one, at least), the information services staff does well to identify those account executives who bring in major contracts and direct their efforts into creating information products and services which can specifically and concretely assist them in procuring further contracts. Such specific techniques as unrequested searches, the identification of information about industry trends, competitive intelligence and the like will establish a serious and mutually beneficial link between the information services group and the very people in the company who are bringing in the business. Likewise, in a charitable organization in which the information services unit exists to support information needs across the board, an emphasis on special information provision for the fundraising and development office can ensure not only that the information unit is recognized for the products and services it provides, it is also more secure than it would otherwise be when predictable economic downturns occur and the charity is forced to consider alternative sources for some of the services for which there is in-house staff.

In her proposal for securing the 'indispensability' of information services, Talcott quotes Barbara Wichser, who sees the challenge for information services managers as two-fold: to first secure management's support and recognition for the information services operation, and then to encourage management's *direct* use of information services, with limited 'filtering' done by a secretary or staff assistant (LaRosa, p. 1). The first of these has already been alluded to, and is discussed more specifically in the following pages. The second challenge is perhaps more problematic, for those 'filters' provided by a good secretary or administrative assistant often exist for a purpose: senior management, not interested in the process that provides the information, is only concerned with the information itself, which means that the staff in the information services unit – and probably the manager of the unit himself or herself – must devise mechanisms for avoiding the secretary or other staff assistants. One time-honored method, of course, is to get to know them, learn what some of their routines are, and learn to 'work around' the routine. One information services manager, for example, might determine exactly when the secretary or assistant is at lunch and leave a message on the senior executive's personal voicemail. Another might seek to track down the executive, knowing that the best time for delivering an impressively packaged information product is when the manager is out in the company, with others, and the entire group has the opportunity to be impressed (and usually is). A third information services manager might have a subordinate invite the secretary or assistant to call for the requested material and then deliver it – appropriately packaged of course, and clearly labelled as coming 'with the compliments of . . .' – to the senior manager in his or her office while the assistant is away. The variations and opportunities are endless, but the point of the exercise is to get the information to the executive with as little interference as possible.

Working with management

In the modern organization, as far as information services are concerned, we have come to recognize that there are, in fact, two 'types' of senior managers who have authority and control over those who are responsible for providing information. The first group is made up of those who understand the value of information and the role that an efficiently managed information services operation plays in an organization. The second group consists of those who must be 'trained' or educated, as gently as possible, in the value of information.

In many respects, today's information services manager is much better off than previous generations of information providers have been. Whether he or she is responsible for records management, organizational archives, the MIS unit, or a specialized library or information center, the information services manager in today's information environment is more likely to have the support and consideration of his or her users, peers, and supervisors than previous generations of information managers, primarily because the proportion of 'enlightened' senior managers (with respect to information services) is higher than it has ever been. Four factors contribute.

Generational differences

Unlike senior directors, officers, and other management personnel in earlier periods of history, today's top managers (regardless of the 'types' of enterprises they manage) are trained to understand the role and value of information in the managerial process. Today's undergraduate and, particularly, graduate management programs emphasize the organization and retrieval of relevant information as a basic component in effective organizational management, and even self-trained managers soon learn that current and precise information is critical in the success or failure of any enterprise they manage. This has not always been the case and, indeed, until the last couple of decades or so (with some notable exceptions), 'information' as a critical and vital component of the management process was quite literally taken for granted. 'Information' was not identified as a product or commodity which required management or control for the successful achievement of the goals of the enterprise. All that has changed now, and most of today's managers recognize the value of strong and efficiently organized information operations. The exceptions, of course, are those senior managers whose training and professional development ended when they assumed management status, and for whom the 'theory' of management, including the requirements for effective and reliable information support systems, was dismissed out of hand. Most of these people are, at this point in time, nearing the end of their careers, and as they leave the workplace, younger managers will assume decision making roles, bringing with them new and more enlightened attitudes about the value of information in the workplace.

New management styles

Despite an amazing array of names and descriptors and a variety of differences between them, the focus in most management 'approaches' these days is on quality, and quality management, by definition, requires particular emphasis on meeting the needs of the recipients in the transaction (the customers) and, in doing so, the empowerment of employees to make decisions that result in higher quality customer interactions. Information is the key to these higher quality endeavors, and today's managers, looking at quality circles, total quality management, benchmarking, re-engineering, and the like, discover that the role of the unit that provides organizational information (whether it is internal or external information is irrelevant) is vital to their success.

Relating to this, of course, is the flattening of the managerial structure, the movement away from the traditional hierarchy to a less rigid, more fluid pursuit of organizational or community objectives. Information services managers who match their own departmental structure to that of the parent enterprise often find that they have unwittingly acquired a more productive, more involved staff. Senior management recognizes when different units are successful, which of course leads to an enhanced relationship between the staff of the individual units so recognized and the executives in the organization. When the information services unit is one of these departments, the value of the unit and its role in contributing to the success of the organization is made clearer to all parties.

Information as a commodity and an asset

Nowadays, the decision makers within any organization or community recognize that timely, accurate and accessible information is key to their success. Senior management personnel now understand that a smooth-flowing information services operation can make the difference between an ordinary, even mediocre, organization and a proactive, fast-paced, and innovative enterprise which is prepared for any opportunity to move forward to even greater success. As a result, information services managers who put forth even the slightest effort to demonstrate how they and their staff contribute to organizational goals are going to be taken seriously by senior managers. These people already know the value of information and information services; they just have to be reminded of it on an ongoing basis.

Information provides the competitive advantage

Whether the parent organization or enterprise is a entity operating in the private sector - attempting to achieve a profit from its efforts - or part of the continually growing public sector, all organizations have competition for what they provide. As senior management has come to recognize the value of competitive intelligence in the achievement of the organization's success, the 'place' of the information services unit providing that information has been considerably enhanced, and management is more inclined to appreciate the services - competitive or otherwise - that the unit brings to the organization.

With these factors contributing to a better appreciation of information and information services, the manager of the information services operation has only to look for opportunities. To be frank, information services and the provision of information, like so much else in our society, are so good and so well done that - for the layperson - they are simply taken for granted. Information, regardless of how valuable it is as a commodity or how necessary it is for beating the competition, is simply not thought about until it is needed, and the information services manager must constantly be putting himself or herself - and the services the information unit provides - forward to identified user groups, targeting non-user groups, management peers in the organization or community, and senior management.

Understanding the partnership

There are, of course, those groups of people to whom the value of the information services operation is minimal, and they, for one reason or another, do not have a very high opinion of information services. Or, more likely, since they do not think about 'information' as a separate concept in their working lives, they may have no opinion at all about the value of information. As information services managers, in determining how we work with senior management in achieving our goals for the information operation, what we have to recognize is that some managers are not in a position to value a specialized library or other information services unit until we teach them these values. Thus when we have a superior (or even a co-worker) who is not very concerned about the success of the information unit, who does not share the information manager's recognition of the value of information services, we have to remind them - in subtle ways - of the 'partnership' agreement into which we have entered. We are there to provide the best services we can (in our terms - we are the information experts) and we have to convince these people to buy into our value system for the library and its services.

A 'partnership' is, in fact, an appropriate framework for looking at the relationships between an information services manager and the senior manager or supervisor to whom he or she reports. If a partner can be defined as a person associated with others in a joint venture or endeavor, certainly what goes on between the manager of an information services operation and his or her immediate superior is a partnership, for each of these people have joined in this workplace association in order to contribute to the success, however defined, of the organization or community which employs them both.

Continuing the analogy, there are certain identifiable characteristics for a successful partnership, and these can be addressed in terms of an information services unit's manager and the executive who has responsibility for the unit. In any partnership, all parties to the activity have common expectations, and this is certainly the case with an information services unit (or, if it is not, it should be, for it is fundamental to the success of the unit within the organization or enterprise which it supports). The mission of the information services department relates directly to the mission of the parent organization or enterprise, and in drawing up the mission statement for the information services unit, the manager of the unit, working in partnership with his or her supervisor, works toward the achievement of common expectations.

Another characteristic of a good partnership is cooperative planning, and the manager of the information services unit will work with his or her manager in planning the operations of the unit, to ensure that they not only match the organizational culture of the environment in which they and their staff work, but that the direction that they set and the policies they establish are, in fact, the best ones for what they are trying to achieve. It is imperative, according to Helen J. Waldron, that the manager of a specialized library or other information services unit has a 'clear picture' of the organizational policies within which the unit will be operating, and it is, of course, one's immediate supervisor to whom one turns, in a partnership arrangement, for learning those policies, simply because, as Waldron has so explicitly stated, 'the quickest way to perdition is to attempt to operate in conflict with those general policies' (Waldron, p. 67). That one's immediate manager provides the most secure source for information about those policies should be self-evident.

A working partnership is characterized by good communications and information exchange, and information services managers who do not establish regular and ongoing briefings with their managers have only themselves to blame when they are perceived, by those managers, as not being part of the management team for the organization or community. Even in those situations in which one's manager is not particularly interested in the operations of the information services unit ('you must take care of the records section - that's why we hired you.'), it behooves the manager of the unit to meet with his or her executive on a regular basis to discuss broader organizational issues that have - or can have - an impact on the management of the information services unit. In this case, at the very least, senior management is kept apprised of the 'big picture' as far as the information unit is concerned and is thus not surprised when changes in direction within the unit must take place. In most cases, however, management is interested in what is going on in the information services unit, just as he or she is interested in the other departments which make up his or her group, and simply needs to be kept informed by the manager of that unit. For most managers, regularly scheduled briefings are best, and while they do not have to be long meetings, it is important that they are recognized as part of the management routine for the information services unit.

In a successful partnership there are two final characteristics which lend themselves well to the relationship between the head of an information services department and his or her manager. These are the joint evaluation of services and products emanating from the information services unit and the establishment of a relationship in which, in these matters, neither 'partner' behaves as superior or inferior to the other. Naturally, one recognizes the superiority of one's manager, and appropriate deference is accorded to that person by virtue of his or her position, but in discussing the goals and objectives of the information services unit, vis-à-vis organizational goals and objectives, a 'levelling-out' must necessarily take place. Both parties must be able to speak frankly and comfortably about the staff, resources, and services being discussed, and mutually agreed-upon standards of performance must be invoked in the evaluation of progress in the information services unit in achieving its goals and objectives.

Working the partnership

It is always useful to step back and attempt an objective look at what one does, and certainly such an exercise is helpful when an information services manager is examining his or her role with senior management. The goal here, it seems, is to look at how we work with senior management and then organize our findings so that we can exploit that partnership to the best advantage of the information services function for which we are responsible. Needless to say, this exploitation, such as it is, comes about without compromising our ideals and standards of service or diminishing in any way the information services unit's commitment to providing those services that best support the achievement of the mission of the organization or community of which we are a part. What we are trying to do, in effect, is to learn what we can about senior management and its perceptions about information and the provision of information services and products within the organization or community, and then, without apology, use what we have learned to direct the efforts of senior management to support the services we have been charged to provide.

In order to determine just *how* we can work with senior management in supporting this 'partnership' (which we have both agreed is good for the parent organization or community of which we are a part), it is a good idea to think about how senior managers think about information and management. Matarazzo, Prusak, and Gauthier made a welcome beginning in their study of corporate libraries in 1990, and among their several conclusions, three are specifically appropriate in this context. Although the survey was limited to specialized libraries and corporate information centers, it seems likely that these same conclusions could be applied to other information services operations. By substituting such terms as 'corporate archives center', 'corporate records office', or 'corporate MIS department', for the term 'library', it becomes apparent that the issues raised here are management issues that affect all information services units (Matarazzo, Prusak, and Gauthier, p. 1).

In the first place, the survey determined that 'librarians evaluate their performance based on standardized library methodologies [and] managers use far different, and often subjective, evaluation criteria'. This gap in evaluative standards is beginning to be addressed, but there are still many organizations in which the specialized librarian, for example, is convinced he is providing good library service because he and his staff process a certain number of technical reports each month, or provide an SDI service to a certain number of company employees, or have the ability to search a certain number of online databases. Senior management, in the same organization, might judge the value of the library on the number of complaints received from dissatisfied users, the amount of staff time allocated to processing those technical reports, or the lengthy turnaround time required for receiving materials requested from notices seen in the SDI distribution. From the management point of view, the library must be seen to operate within the framework of the organization as a whole, and when it does not, when evaluative criteria for the library do not match those used elsewhere in the organization, conflict arises.

Such situations relate naturally to the second of the study's conclusions, that 'there is little managerial consensus on how the library adds specific value to the firm's performance or how value should be measured'. To gain a managerial consensus, those who are responsible for libraries and other information services operations must begin to insist, as Ann Lawes has suggested (see Chapter Five), on mutually agreed-upon performance standards early in the game. Think about, for example, the information center in a trade association, created to provide technical reports and standards to the members of the association. The services of the information center are advertised to the members as a free benefit of membership, and many members take advantage of the presence of the information center at their organization's headquarters.

Seeking to justify to the association's governing board the costs for maintaining and staffing the information center, senior management asked the director of the information center to put together a set of performance standards that would relate to how the services of the center affect the work of the users. Since most requests for services are received via telephone, fax, or e-mail, and an introductory 'interview' is part of the procedure for members who wish to request information and services, the director of the center, working with her immediate manager, created a short list of questions to be added to the interview. Asking such questions as 'would you mind telling us – without revealing any proprietary information – how you will use this material?' provided a considerable amount of information which senior management could then take to the governing board and demonstrate the value of the information center to the members of the association. Admittedly, most of the responses are anecdotal and therefore require some commitment of staff time for analysis and compilation, but the rewards of having such information available to the decision makers in the organization (coupled with the newly enhanced role of the information center within the organizational structure) make the effort more than worthwhile.

A third finding of the Matarazzo, Prusak, and Gauthier study was that 'librarians have little say on the firm's information policies and mission' and, sadly, that few of those who participated in the study 'could state what exact function the library performs within the firm's information structure'. Obviously, the day of the integrated information structure has not arrived, despite the efforts of many leaders in the information services field. The reasons probably have to do with the distinctions management makes between the internally generated materials which are frequently referred to in a variety of ways (the organization's records), and the 'external' material that is brought into the organization through the specialized library or information center. Until recently, most senior managers have seen the two types of information as unrelated when, in fact, most of those conducting research need to determine, before they seek a piece of information, which unit of the organization to go to for the information. In some cases, the user may need organizational archives, for older records, reports, etc. In other cases, current records are required and, of course, for many projects, materials and information must be gathered from outside the organization. Integrating these varied information requirements and a universal automation services department into a centralized operation that supports all its component parts is of course an idealized desire on the part of many senior managers, yet even in those organizations in which steps have been taken to create such a scheme, the input of the organization's library staff is most often not sought (and few organizations have a professionally trained librarian as 'Chief Information Officer').

Nevertheless, there is an opportunity for information services professionals to be involved in the establishment and management of organizational information policy, but it must of necessity be a self-asserted opportunity. Librarians and other information services employees understand the information function and they understand the service concepts connected with quality service provision, so it is up to them to seek out ways in which they can influence management in this direction. A useful example can be found in the changes that were incorporated at a medium-sized museum. Nearly one hundred years old, the museum had over the years accumulated a vast array of archival material which, in a recent reorganization, was moved to an off-site location. The museum library, automated some years ago and utilizing a standard turn-key system acquired at the time, primarily serves the curatorial staff, although some service is offered to graduate students at a local university and to the general public (with some limitations, as the museum library is not a 'public' library, per se). The records management function in the museum's administrative department had never been automated, and none of the records in the registrar's office were available electronically. In a happy stroke of recognition, when the museum's management staff decided to seek funding to automate its records activities, a member of the Board of Trustees (a librarian, incidentally) remembered that the museum library was automated and suggested that the librarian be invited to sit on a committee to study an overall automation program. As a result of her expertise and interest (as well as her own ability to bring up the names of vendors, consultants, and others in the information industry who could be useful to the museum), by the time the museum's management was ready to seek bids from vendors, a decision had been made to integrate, as much as possible, all operations into one system. There were difficulties, of course. The project turned out to be a larger one than originally envisioned, and more expensive, but the results, as far as service to the information seekers was concerned, were and continue to be very positive, and the museum now has a system that can take it into the next twenty years or so with considerable comfort and ease.

Recognizing how senior management thinks about information services is useful, but for maximum benefit, that recognition must be connected with the level of service – that is, the quality of service – provided by the information services unit. Thomas W. Shaughnessy has suggested that it is the effectiveness of the information services manager which is all important here, for that effectiveness 'influences perceptions and attitudes of peers, other department heads, even users', and these perceptions and attitudes, in turn, influence the allocation of resources, the information service unit's relationships and involvements with its service community, and the centrality of the role of the information service unit vis-à-vis the larger organization (Shaughnessy, p. 9). Consequently, positive relationships must be built up between information services staff and these other groups, especially senior management, and every effort should be made to change perceptions whenever the information services manager or other staff recognizes a lack of interest, lack of esteem, etc. about the products and services provided by the unit.

In working with senior management, there are a number of basic rules which should be observed. Shaughnessy has identified five 'tips' for understanding one's immediate supervisor, and they are worth repeating here:

1. How the boss reacts to stress.

2. Whether the boss is a reader or listener.

3. Keeping the boss informed. He/she is not a mind reader (never hide problems).

4. No surprises (from the boss's point of view: 'a pleasant surprise is an oxymoron!').

5. Boss's focus of planning: his/her assumptions about the organization, his/her priorities, timeframe and motivations.

Shaughnessy has also pointed out that it is important for the information services manager to develop an understanding and appreciation of the multiple roles a senior management employee must play. For many in information services work, the focus on the delivery of information services and products is so intense that the 'larger picture' is ignored and for senior management, of course, it is this 'larger picture' which is the primary concern. While the manager of the information services unit does not necessarily have to understand and attempt to relate to every other operation for which his or her manager is responsible, it is, nevertheless, an important consideration. Being aware of the demands on one's manager and having some interest in and sympathy for the overall operations which demand that manager's attention all combine to enable the information services manager to organize and coordinate his or her own activities in such a way that both parties find mutually beneficial.

For some, the problems of working with senior management and other supervisors have more to do with what they know (or do not know) than what they are. There is a tendency, it seems, for information services personnel to regard it as something of a professional failing on the part of their senior managers when they do not understand or express particular interest in their work ('my boss doesn't like libraries' is a standard lament, along with 'he/she doesn't know what we do in the library.'). As part of this, many information services professionals have difficulty with the idea of reporting to nonprofessionals, that is, to people who do not have their training in and understanding of the information function. David Drake wrote about this and noted that it is not such an unusual phenomenon: '. . . In many large organizations, specialists report to generalists who have some idea of what their subordinates do, but little genuine understanding of how they do it. (Drake, p. 152).

It is Drake's contention, and he is correct in this assertion, that information services practitioners need to recognize that their managers' attitudes were formed *before* they became managers. They had their own vision of libraries and other information services, and the job of the information services manager is to enhance that vision or, as Drake puts it, 'at least bring it into alignment with reality'.

What the library or information services manager wants to do, of course, is change those perceptions, so that senior management does, indeed, have a more realistic understanding of the nature (and value) of information services work. To do that, according to Drake, requires an honest recognition of two realities:

1. An understanding that the boss 'does not and never will have the in-depth understanding and appreciation' of the library/information services unit that you do.

2. An understanding that the boss already has a definite image or perception of the library/information services unit.

Accepting these 'realities', which is, in effect, accepting the lay person's usual view of information services, enables the manager of the information services unit to understand some of the reasoning behind some managerial decisions and, hopefully, to determine exactly which strategies to use in working with that manager.

The working relationship between senior management and those who provide information services has been an ongoing concern for many years, probably not so much connected with information services itself, as a subject, as with the working relationships between *any* middle management personnel and their senior managers. Certainly the debate will continue as long as information services managers are struggling to provide the highest levels of quality service for their users while their senior management is attempting to keep costs, staff, and other resources at an acceptable level. The situation creates a delicious tension, and while there are no guarantees for success in this endeavor, Judy Labovitz has identified what she calls three 'keys' for working successfully with senior management (Labovitz, pp. 10–11).

Keeping your options open is Labovitz's first admonition. Being option oriented should be automatic, for it broadens your horizons and, as Labovitz notes, 'keeps you from becoming stale'. As important as anything else, how-ever, is that when circumstances change and, despite your agreements with senior management, you do not get what has been promised or what you have been counting on, you do not fall apart. You 'already have a new plan of action' which you can refer to and which can, in many circumstances, enable you to provide at least some portion of the service you had planned, even if you cannot provide it at the level you had originally sought.

Labovitz comes in with all the other management advisors with her second 'key' to success in working with management. 'Measure, measure, measure,' she writes, emphasizing the need to use statistics regularly and to compare what you do and how you do it with standards that you and your manager have agreed upon (including such factors as cost and how long it takes to complete the tasks you have set out to measure). Despite the reference earlier to the fact that most managements often use subjective criteria for measuring performance in information services, this does not necessarily mean that they *want* to do so. All good management is based on quantifiable, objective measures, and by combining statistical measures (when appropriate) with effectiveness measures, the information services manager establishes a working relationship with management that is mutually rewarding. The playing field has been levelled, so to speak, and with both parties speaking the same language, the credibility of the manager of the information services unit is solidly established.

There is little to disagree with in Labovitz's third direction: 'politics and self-interest are the name of the current and only game in town . . . if you want to be successful, you must learn the game'. Despite our reluctance to do so, 'playing politics' is in fact a healthy approach to information services management, and when politics is combined with a healthy dose of self-interest, better provision of information will result. Why? Because those information services managers who learn the political game, who recognize the value of self-interest in putting themselves and their operations forward are the ones who will obtain the resources to provide the services they are there to provide. Make no mistake about it: despite woeful cries from many administrators and senior management that 'there is no more money', in fact, if one looks around the organization, there are sections, departments, and even entire divisions which are well-funded and given the support they need to provide a level of service that has been agreed upon between themselves and senior management. For the clever information services manager (especially one who is constantly being encouraged to 'improve' or 'enhance' services but not being given the resources to do so), an in-depth study of those 'successful' departments and an analysis of how their work is funded can be a beneficial exercise. While there may, indeed, be no 'more' money, there is money being disbursed throughout the organization. What the innovative information services manager must do is learn to play the game of politics and self-interest, as Labovitz has recommended, and find out how to get some of that money for information services. If there is no *more* money, you find some somewhere else that you can arrange to apply to your own department's needs. It is done all the time, but it requires assertiveness, sometimes audacity, and certain skill in playing 'the only game in town'.

This discussion leads, naturally enough, to the point that must be made as we attempt to understand the relationships that grow up between information services managers and the senior management personnel to whom they report. Joel Barker, among others, talks about 'shifting paradigms', and for information services employees, the most difficult paradigm to shift is the one that confuses quality service, in the provision of information, with service as practiced in traditional librarianship, education and social work. In fact, it is almost a confusion between 'service' and 'servitude', for while information services managers and their staff are required (often without appropriate resources, alas) to offer the best levels of quality service to their information customers, the menial tasks observed by many users in a traditional library setting lead them to place those information providers, in their own perceptions, in a subservient sort of role, thus depriving them of the respect and authority they deserve. What must happen, it seems clear, is that information services practitioners of all types must reassess some of their philosophical underpinnings, especially those that have been carried over from earlier generations, to determine if they are, in fact, appropriate for effective information delivery today.

If there is to be an attitudinal change, a 'shifting of paradigms', an embracing of a new 'philosophy' for information services, perhaps it will appropriately come from a recognition of who we are, as information services providers, and who *really* 'calls the shots', as far as support of information services is concerned. Lawrence White has set the stage: we work and function, he has written, as part of:

> An economic system which is essentially a private enterprise system. It is based ultimately on notions of (and rules and laws about) private ownership of property and on notions of personal gain. Now, you can call this last concept 'greed', you can call it 'profit'. Choose your own word here. I will use a relatively neutral term and call it 'personal gain'. The economy is largely composed of firms producing goods and services and selling those goods and services in the market. The prices for those goods and services in the market – their value in the market – are more or less set by supply and demand. (White, pp. 17–18)

If we, as information services providers, accept White's definition of information as 'the provision of new knowledge or understanding to someone who didn't have it before', do we not have an obligation to carry to our own managers the concept that the information we manage and control is unique, that it has 'value'? Certainly if we are successful in doing this, in looking at (and analyzing) the products and services we supply as candidates for 'supply and demand', the information services unit takes on an entirely new meaning within the organizational framework. In some organizations, of course, the change has already taken place, as some specialized libraries and records management units have taken on the 'just-in-time' (as opposed to the 'just-in-case') approach to information provision, acquiring the specific information materials as needed instead of stockpiling materials 'in case' they are needed.

In summary, we can turn again to Phillip Morton, for he has identified the steps in the process. Following his three fundamental criteria, the information services manager can be responsible for building 'an information organization that has realized the vital linkage between information and knowledge' (Morton, pp. 77–79).

Morton's three steps begin with an understanding of what it is we do as information services managers, and that understanding acknowledges that the product we work with is important within the organization or community of which the information service operation is a part:

> First, and foremost, we are establishing the credibility of our product – information – as part of effective decision making. We are also working from the assumption that the value of our information technology is tied to our own ability to communicate about it.

And like Labovitz and many others, Morton looks to measurement as basic to establishing the value of information services within an organization or community:

> A second fundamental is an understanding of the support role information people play and the knowledge that their work is *always* measured by line managers. *Measurement* is the key word. . . . All staff functions are sustained by their value to the line organization. The personnel must be willing to risk having their services measured by others. This is crucial because it is the only way line management has of assessing the value of staff services. Information organizations need internal measures that are meaningful to line managers, not ones understood only by other information specialists.

According to Morton, there are very pragmatic reasons why information services managers should be willing – and even anxious – to participate in organizational performance management activities.

'When an information organization is measured and when that measurement comes up on the positive side then, and only then, is there a good chance top management will reward its performance,' Morton writes, and he goes on to list the rewards:

1. Money.

2. Technology.

3. Opportunity for professional growth.

4. Support for operating procedures that strengthen the acquisition of information.

He points out, however, that such rewards do not come without a 'price', as he calls it, and that is, on the part of the information services manager, 'the acceptance of managerial responsibility'. Morton contends that such responsibility is not familiar to most information services practitioners, and his third fundamental criterion for success as an information services manager is that information professionals 'acknowledge their managerial responsibilities, step up to them and function as true managers in every sense of the word'. Such behavior, Morton suggests, has five 'basic dimensions in an information organization':

1. The manager must see 'information *and* communication in their broadest contexts, to know, understand, and deal not only with the technology of information handling, but also with the behavioral characteristics of users and the opportunities information presents to increase the productivity of its customers'.

2. The manager must stimulate the information staff 'to get out of their own work areas, to go onto their customers' turf, find out what is going on and how they can help. All good support organizations and their people must develop the skill of interacting with users, identifying their problems through this interaction, and developing creative solutions'.

3. Managers must expand services through the use of new technology, '*not* through more people'.

4. Managers must plan by providing both 'evolutionary and revolutionary programs and services'.

5. Managers must use other staff organizations 'to supplement and expand the information staff's expertise wherever and whenever possible'.

References

Barker, Joel A. *Discovering the Future: The Business of Paradigms*. Lake Elmo, MN: Infinity Ltd. Inc, 1985.

Drake, David. 'When your boss isn't a librarian.' *American Libraries*. February, 1990.

Echelman, Shirley. 'Libraries are businesses too.' *Special Libraries*. 65, October/November, 1974.

Ferguson, Elizabeth and Mobley, Emily R. *Special Libraries at Work*. Hamden, CT: Library Professional Publications, 1984.

Kok, John. '"Now that I'm in charge, what do I do?' Six rules about running a special library for the new library manager. *Special Libraries*. 71 (4), December, 1980.

Labovitz, Judy. 'Managing a special library.' *Journal of Library Administration*. 6 (3), Fall, 1985.

LaRosa, Sharon. 'In pursuit of partnership.' *MLS: Marketing Library Services*. 7 (3), April/May, 1993.

Matarazzo, James. *Closing the Corporate Library*. Washington, DC: Special Libraries Association, 1984.

Matarazzo, James, Prusak, Laurence, and Gauthier, Michael R. *Valuing*

Corporate Libraries: A Survey of Senior Managers. Washington, DC: Special Libraries Association, 1990.

Morton, Phillip W. 'The information manager: a link in effective organizational decision making.' *Managing the Electronic Library: Papers of the 1982 Conference of the Library Management Division of the Special Libraries Association*, edited by Michael Koenig. New York: Special Libraries Association, 1983.

Mount, Ellis. *Special Libraries and Information Centers: An Introductory Text*. Washington, DC: Special Libraries Association, 1991.

Paul, Meg. 'Improving service provision.' *The Australian Library Journal*. 22 (10), November, 1991.

Shaughnessy, Thomas W. 'Making the boss more effective.' *Journal of Library Administration*. 8 (2), Summer, 1987.

Talcott, Ann. 'Indispensable or expendable? Making yourself valuable to your organization.' Unpublished paper presented at the Special Libraries Association Northeast Regional Conference, November 3, 1993.

Waldron, Helen J. 'The business of running a special library.' *Special Libraries*. 62, February, 1972.

White, Lawrence. 'The sensible economist's guide to the economics of information.' *The Economics of Information: Proceedings of the Twentieth Annual Symposium Sponsored by the Alumni and Faculty of the Rutgers Graduate School of Library and Information Studies, April 3, 1981*. Jefferson, NC: McFarland & Company, 1982.

Chapter Ten
Identifying the political team

The basic premise of this book is that information services practitioners cannot, by themselves, ensure that support for their work is provided. We are talking here about tangible support, resources to do the work, as has been said before, that they are charged to do. In most cases, these information professionals (librarians, records managers, archivists, computer programmers, information brokers and the like) are not in positions of authority with regard to the provision of resources for information services, and they must rely on others to give them what they need. No matter how good one is as a manager, say, of a corporate information center or institutional records department, the information services unit, the information center or records department will always be in competition with other units in the organization for organizational support, and the manager of the unit simply is not able to do it alone. He or she must have others who will support what the information services unit is doing, and these political supporters, advocates, must be identified and exploited.

There are, of course, any number of reasons for this phenomenon, many of which have been explored elsewhere in this book. In the final analysis, however, the real explanation lies in the finances of the organization or community which supports the information services unit. Richard A. Willner, writing about the proliferation of information technology in corporations since the decade of the eighties, has put the matter in perspective:

> While the technology permitted information professionals to add much more value, it also greatly increased information expense. Rising expense made financial management the fundamental library management competency, while intensifying top management pressure on the library more generally. (Willner, p. 232)

Therefore, the primary responsibility of the manager of an information services unit must be to find those political advocates who recognize the success of the information operation in its financial management and who will, with or without being asked, play a role in encouraging support for the information services unit within the organization. As is clearly evident from the preceding chapter, the employees who make up the various management strata are singularly significant as candidates for this role. At the same time, supportive users and peers within the organization or community must also be aligned, either wittingly or unwittingly, to provide political support for the information services unit. Finally, the information services manager himself or herself, working as a member of project committees or teams, provides an unrecognized influence in setting up advocacy relationships within the organization or community.

Managers into advocates*

For those information services professionals who would succeed, management support is essential. Yet managers are the one group who are perfectly willing to provide laudatory 'lip-service' about the value of a library, archives center, or other information services unit, yet are the same people who, when the crunch comes, find that information services are just another overhead line in the organizational budget and, as the scenario usually goes, 'since it doesn't bring in any profit it is a drain on the company'. Changing these managers' perceptions about information services is vital if the information services unit is to have proper support. These people must be targeted as potential advocates.

David Drake has pointed out that the manager of the information services unit must remember that senior managers are not information professionals and that in practically all cases, the information services manager will be reporting to a person who not only is not part of the information services field but who, more than likely, sees that field as simply a means to an end; the information services unit, from the management point of view, exists only to assist the members of the organization in the achievement of organizational goals. With this recognition in mind, as well as the management expectations described in Chapter Six (O'Donnell), the manager of the information services unit can set out to acquire what Charles Bauer has identified as 'management acknowledgement', that is, the appropriate recognition of the value of the information services unit to the organization and a willingness to provide the support and the resources for the successful operation of the unit (Bauer, p. 216).

---

*Much of the material here originally appeared, in slightly different form, in a section called 'Using Management' in a chapter on advocacy and political support in *Managing the New One-Person Library* (Bowker-Saur, 1992). I am indebted to the editors at Bowker-Saur and to my co-author of that book, Joan Williamson, for permission to use this material here.

There are specific steps the manager of the information services unit can take to create interest on the part of senior management in the work that is being done in the unit, and these very basic steps should be considered:

- *Establish personal contact* There are times when it is to the advantage of the manager of the information services unit to know something about a supervisor's personal interests, what some of his or her own professional concerns are. With this knowledge, the information services manager and his or her staff can direct materials, ideas, or comments to the manager without being asked.

- *Communicate easily* One of the greatest failings of middle managers is that they often seem intimidated by senior management and fail to establish regular communications patterns. It is very important to have established communications routines in place, so that the manager of the information services unit can feel comfortable bringing up subjects which may or may not be of specific interest, but which, for the good of the organization, must be discussed openly and frankly. An example might be a particularly troublesome user who frequently seems just on the verge of making trouble. If the manager of the unit has mentioned it casually from time to time to his/her own supervisor, if there is an explosion from the user, senior management is not caught by surprise.

- *Know when to pull back* There are times when, even in the most supportive of situations, a manager might have had just about enough from the library, archives, or other information services unit. Even if that unit is his or her favorite part of the organizational operation (and that is frequently the case, since libraries and information centers are comforting and intellectually rewarding to many managers, and they gravitate to them as comfortable retreats), it is nevertheless, only one of several areas of responsibility for this manager. If the information services manager is always coming to this senior manager for support or advice, it might be withheld simply in order to close the discussion. For example, a records manager who has been asked to draw up the specifications for a new word processing system for the department would be wise not to be asking opinions of his or her senior manager about specific features or special services of targeted systems. If the records manager figures out what is needed and presents management with a plan, approval for the package and support for a request for it is more likely.

At this point, and related to this idea, it seems appropriate to touch on a couple of practical approaches for working with senior management. One comes from Judy Labovitz, in which she presents a rather tough but interesting point of view about managers:

One of my secrets when dealing with upper managements is realizing that they (1) don't like making decisions, (2) do want people to think of them as decision makers, and (3) don't have time to read a lot. (Labovitz, p. 6)

Therefore, Labovitz suggests, in presenting proposals to senior management, it is important that they be presented as succinctly as possible. Three should always be offered, with of course an explanation of why the option the information services manager wants to implement is the one that will work the best.

Similarly, Thomas Shaughnessy has tips on how to deliver bad news to senior management. Instead of saying 'here's the problem. What do we do?' – which implies that it is the manager's problem and he or she is responsible for fixing it, Shaughnessy recommends the approach that says, 'here's the problem and here are two or three suggested solutions I've come up with for us to think about'. This latter approach, of course, implies that the problem is a mutual problem, and that the solution will be arrived at mutually (Shaughnessy, p. 9).

There are other specific steps for ensuring management support, both having to do with attitudes that are well within the control of the manager of the information services unit.

- *Don't create trouble unnecessarily* It is the information services manager's responsibility to manage the unit. He or she knows it and so does senior management. If advice is sought from senior management in every situation, not only does the manager of the information unit put his or her professionalism on the line, he or she runs the risk of conveying an impression of being an inferior manager. The information services manager should save high-level consultations for major problems that he or she doesn't feel competent to handle or skilled enough to solve. For example, if a user is complaining that the information center does not offer a particular service which is beyond the resources and scope of the information center, the information services manager must take it upon himself or herself to explain in reasonable terms why the service is not offered.

- *Stroke* This might seem like a contradiction to the above, but it is really part of the requirement for maintaining good relations in the workplace. For some reason, some information services workers have a very self-effacing, humble attitude about themselves and their work and seem to want to be ignored, to be invisible, when they are working in a library or other information services unit. Actually, just the opposite attitude is called for, and the information services manager and his/her staff must recognize the importance of being courteous to any senior manager who comes into the unit, to show respect (and even, occasionally, deference) to that person's position. This is not to suggest a mindless kind of subservience on the part of information services staff, for that does not belong in a professional situation, but if the demeanor of the manager of the information services unit and his/her staff conveys a certain courteous regard for senior management personnel, those people are going to feel more comfortable about being in the information services unit and have a more positive attitude about the work that is done there. (Berner and St. Clair, 1990, pp. 48–49)

As an addendum to the concept of 'stroking' (and perhaps to the 'personal contact' idea as well), we should look at the role the information services unit plays in terms of how we might generate enthusiasm and interest in some of the techniques we use for information work. We might think about exploiting management interest in some of the new things that he or she, as a manager in the nineties, must be concerned with:

> More and more, managers are hearing about amazing technological advances. They read about them in their management journals and in *The New York Times*, they watch programs about them on public television and, worst of all, they observe junior staff members – computer whizzes all! – becoming increasingly adept at finding obscure information. In corporate libraries, in records management departments and other information services units in their companies, these managers are finding that – as far as information is concerned – the sky's the limit. They can ask these people for anything and they'll get it.
>
> Nevertheless, some managers are finding that they want to participate in the process themselves. Not all of them, of course, and not all the time, but certainly some of these managers would appreciate an invitation to a new product presentation or a 'brown-bag' lunch for discussing a new concept or idea. For many of these managers, especially some of the senior managers who are not connected with the information services section in any way, such an opportunity for more information could be useful and productive.
>
> Of course information management is the responsibility of the information services staff, but senior management is interested, wants to know what's going on, and with very little encouragement can be brought into the 'information picture' within the organization. Even if nothing else happens, the information services staff might find itself winning over some true 'converts' in these senior management people. It could be worth a try. (*InfoManage*, p. 5)

Suggesting that technology might be the next place for eliciting management interest in the library or other information services unit, Andrew Berner wrote about this concept in 1989. Berner had read that the manager of the future will need specialized knowledge directly applicable to selected tasks, and that this knowledge will be combined with hands-on familiarity with advanced information techniques. Berner went further, suggesting that demonstrating to management that the library or other information services unit is the logical organizational focus for developing a working knowledge of technology, and he offered four approaches for the manager of the information services unit to use in creating management interest in this work:

1.   Talk to managers on a one-to-one basis. Let them know that you and your staff are available to provide this needed information to them.

2.   Send memos to those you think would benefit from an increased knowledge of information technology, and explain to them just how they will benefit and how the information services staff can help. Include as many senior management as you can, including people in top positions (directors, for example).

3.   If the information services operation publishes a newsletter, or if the organization has a house organ, include an article on the benefits of technology and the role of the information services unit in helping managers secure that understanding. Do not simply distribute other people's thoughts on the subject. Be sure that you explain to managers how the library can help them gain this vital knowledge.

4.   If you are sufficiently knowledgeable in the area, or someone on your staff is, hold seminars for managers of the subject of information technology. If you don't feel confident enough to do this yourself, or it isn't possible to do it through your unit, check the professional literature to find out when seminars are being offered, and be sure to announce them to management. (Berner, p. 4)

In any discussion of advocacy for an information services unit, and of influencing management to play an advocacy role for the unit, primary, of course, is the level of service provided specifically for management in meeting their information needs. How good this service is naturally reflects on the quality and the standards conveyed by the staff of the information services unit, to say nothing of the influence that it has on the perceptions of the very managers themselves. Ann Willard and Patricia Morrison, in writing about the subtle distinctions between the work of an information specialist and a corporate librarian, recognize the opportunity this provides for the information services unit, regardless of the kind of information provided by the unit:

> Politics and economics, both on a corporate and global scale, greatly influence needs for service in the corporate library. If the president of the company makes a request, his or her request receives priority: the users of a corporate library are not created equal. Because of the competitive nature of business, information must often be obtained immediately, even at a high cost. Priorities are dynamic, and the information specialist must be able to drop one task to perform another.
>
> Service in a company library can be divided into three functions. The first is current awareness, that is, keeping the company informed of important new

developments. The second is compiling and packaging information so that it is relevant, organized, and useful. The third is applying traditional information resources and skills to satisfy requirements unique to the organization. (Willard and Morrison, p. 273)

The role of an information services unit within an organization, according to Labovitz, is two-fold, and both of these can be exploited by the interested information services manager for the benefit of the operation he or she has responsibility for. Labovitz notes that not only does the unit have an obligation for the cost-effective provision of information, it also has a responsibility for the management of information, which goes beyond the usual special services such as selective dissemination of information (SDI) and current awareness. 'Today's executives,' Labovitz writes, 'cannot handle the information deluge. They need an advisor who can assist them in evaluating what is important for them to keep up with and in what format, and then work with them to decide how best to do this. The task is ongoing because new material/formats continually appear and executives' information needs periodically change.' (Labovitz, p. 10).

Carrying this idea even further, William T. Esrey, speaking on productivity and the role of information services in the achievement of productivity at the 1991 White House Conference on Library and Information Services, spoke of the information services providers as 'information counselors' and spoke very specifically about the function that those information counselors perform:

> As a businessman, I would say the people who manage the distillation and distribution of information in this country play an absolutely critical role in helping American businesses reach a higher quality of productivity and compete on a global plane.
>
> Notice I said higher *quality* of productivity. I believe there's going to be a greater focus on the quality of products and services from here on out, because quality, more than quantity, is going to be the hallmark of successful competitors in the future. It's the quality that makes you stand out.
>
> There's no exception when it comes to libraries.
>
> It's pretty obvious that the information counselor's job is going to get tougher, even more sophisticated, as information plays a bigger and bigger role in productivity, and becomes more integrated with the basic management process. (Esrey, pp. 45–46)

Finally, we look at the levels of professional service as outlined by Barbara Denton in a paper she delivered to an international conference on business information and we think about how the provision of information services and products at these various levels enables information services managers to influence senior managers to be advocates and political supporters for the library, records management unit, institutional archives, or other information services unit for which he or she is responsible. We are now, Denton says, working as information *intermediaries*, information *analysts*, or as information *counselors*, and each of these levels of service requires a different focus. Information analysts, for example, add the *evaluation* of data to the information process and accept responsibility for the information provided, while at the next level, information consultants work with information customers to provide access to the wealth of resources available for them, regardless of format (EBIC '94, p. 2).

There are, then, opportunities for the manager of an information services unit to work with senior management to interest them in the information operation and the work that is done there. A certain assertiveness is required, of course, and there will be those executives who will not react to the overtures of the information services manager or his or her staff, but most people are flattered to be invited to learn more about something that is, to them, very esoteric and unusual, or to discover that they, as the recipients of the information products and services provided by the information unit, can have the highest quality services made available to them. If the manager of the information services unit is willing to make the effort, the rewards to the unit, in terms of support, managerial interest and increased resources to do the work, will make the effort worthwhile.

Supportive users and peers

For many information services professionals, the obvious source for political advocates for the information operation is the body of users who make up the information unit's normal constituency. Certainly these people should be exploited, especially when they have conveyed to the information services staff that they are pleased with the results of the work that the staff provided, but there are others whose efforts can equally be taken advantage of by the information services manager who, with his or her staff, is attuned to recognizing these people. In all cases, efforts must be made to convey to these people that the information services unit is a valuable and important part of the organization and community which supports it, and to enlist their services in changing the perceptions of others who do not yet recognize that value.

Naturally the primary focus for any advocacy or political support group will be those users who know of the value of the information services unit, who take advantage of its services with some regularity, and who are known to the staff of the unit to be satisfied – or even pleased – with the information products and services that they receive from the information services unit. Determining who these satisfied customers are is part of the unit's ordinary performance measurement and evaluation process, for as follow-up surveys are conducted (whether in person, by telephone, through written or faxed communications), a body of people will emerge who have indicated consistent satisfaction with the services they received. It is up to the manager of the information services unit to establish a process though which she and/or selected staff members 'target' such customers and make every effort to ensure that the services they receive are not only up to the high standards that they have come to expect, but to take the time and energy to go beyond those levels for 'value-added' services specifically designed for those customers. When this happens, these people are not only willing to discuss the information services unit and its needs with others, but to put themselves forward – often without being asked – to recognize the information operation as vital to their work and to their contribution to the organization or community as a whole.

An example can be found in a mid-range public relations firm, in which the manager of the information center is also in charge of hiring and training the annual crop of interns that are employed by the firm in order to help them establish their careers. The manager of the information center has determined that a particular account executive requires a specific piece of information as early as possible each day, so she has devised a method by which the first intern reporting to work, at 8.45am, procures the information and hand delivers it to the account executive's office as he comes in, at 9.00am, thus not only giving him the information he requires, but establishing that his need is a serious one that justifies the 'extra' value that is provided. Needless to say, this account executive has nothing but good to say about the information center and in fact is quite often very open in his praise of the services of the center with respect to his work. As he has the ear of the firm's managing director and works closely with him on several specific accounts, the value of the information center and the excellence of its staff is indirectly conveyed (and directly, when necessary) to the highest authority in the company.

Another example of the 'satisfied user/advocate' customer is the recipient of a survey (a *brief* survey) asking how much of her time is saved by having a library, records management unit, archives facility, etc. onsite, as opposed to offsite storage. Most of these people who work regularly within the organization do not think about how their time is spent, but when they are asked to quantify exactly how much time they save by having the facility at hand, most of them are surprised at the query and delighted to give some attention to the matter. In doing so, of course, they unconsciously give value to the facility itself, for without it their work would be more difficult. They are, so to speak, put in a 'receptive' frame of mind about the value of having the information services unit as part of the organizational framework within which they operate on a daily basis, and it becomes important to them to recognize the value of the facility and its services.

There are others, too, who can be, if developed, valuable advocates for the library or other information services operation. They are the people who might be called the 'naturals', as far as information is concerned. It was Doris Bolef who first identified these people, in an essay she wrote about marketing the special library to an identified user group and noted that it is not unusual to find support among the users themselves:

... Selling the library can take on several forms. Often a group of patrons forms a 'belt system' around a library. Usually highly literate and interested in libraries, having used them all their lives, these patrons provide support essential to the library's well-being. They help open the channels of communication both ways, formal and informal. They serve as sources of invaluable information to the [library] manager about the organization and where it is going. At the same time, through them the [library] manager can spread the word about the library's programmes, especially new or changed ones. Such patrons should be continually courted and the number increased with no departmental favoritism. It goes without saying that members of this group receive a higher level of service. (Bolef, p. 59)

Naturally these are people to be exploited as advocates for the information services unit, and they must be sought out and encouraged (although, with this group, it does not take much encouragement) to speak for the library or other information services unit, to convey to senior management the value of the unit, and to keep others in the organization and community alerted about their strong attachment to the information unit and how its presence affects their lives.

Another important group of advocates, although not so common in the business information community, are those people who might be referred to as 'friends and other connections', for these are the users of the information services unit who not only recognize the value of the unit for their work, but take it upon themselves to make others aware as well. Of course in the public library community, and even in some academic situations, it is not uncommon to have a formal support group known as, say, 'The Friends of the XYZ Library', or 'The Associates of the XYZ University Library'. These people, highly organized (they even have their own section of the American Library Association) make great efforts in providing financial support for underfunded libraries and can often be seen at the forefront of funding battles between public library trustees or university library administrators and the funding authorities who are, of necessity, not providing the level of funding the libraries' managers are seeking. In this case, the advocacy is already in place, and, in the public and academic library sectors, very successful.

Such friends groups are, as noted, not so evident in the other branches of information services, primarily because of the more 'private' nature of those information activities, but they are, nevertheless, not unknown. In recent years, several private libraries have organized friends groups, and while these groups have often come about because of financial need, they actually produce larger, advocacy results which are invariably beneficial for the library. One such activity has been described:

If financing is predetermined, and there is no opportunity for additional funding, where does the innovative library manger go for the funds needed for reorganization? He or she goes to the users. Most people who use a private library do so because the library provides something they cannot get elsewhere, be it a unique collection, a beautiful space, a particular ambiance they can't find in more public institutions, or any of the variety of special things they find in the library. These users can be effectively utilized. They can be invited to join a 'friends-of-the-library' organization, and they will, more than likely, be flattered that you have asked them to become involved. If you initiate this effort (which we highly recommend), a private library does call for some special handling, unlike some of the public library efforts along these lines. For example, even the most independent private library will not be appropriately served if the new friends group is formed for the sole purpose of raising money (although this is certainly a major consideration). In a private library, users are presumably already paying (directly or indirectly) to use the library. Some additional entice- ment must be provided for them to form a friends group, and this can be anything from having each additional contribution pay for a book added to the collection in the member's name, to programs, lectures, speeches, and social events that bring members together based on their mutual interest in the library. (Berner and St. Clair, 1987, p. 26)

Even in the corporate and research information fields, such activities, while much more informal, have been known to meet with some success. In these cases, however, the process has been more along the lines of the creation of an 'advisory' committee, with some not-too-well-defined responsibility to work with the manager of the library or other information services unit, usually having to do with the acquisition of materials or the discussion and design of specific services for the unit. In effect, the group functions more as an information 'focus group', so to speak, than in any formal way. In some organizations, of course, there has been established a formal library, archives, or records management committee and these groups, strictly advisory by definition, exist to work with the managers of the specific information services units to ensure that the materials, policies, and operations of the unit match the needs of the organization of which it is a part. These are not managerial units (or they should not be, and when they are, efforts must be made to return them to their advisory role) and, as has been keenly observed by both White (p. 104) and Katayama (p. 44), the committee does not exist to make policy decisions or establish priorities. Managerial responsibility for the information unit rests with the unit's manager and must continue to do so, despite the existence of a committee. The committee, by virtue of its very existence, is there to serve specifically as an advocate for the information unit and its services and, with respect to the unit itself, solely in an advisory capacity.

In discussing advocacy for an information services unit, an extension of the concept of users as advocates is team participation, which was alluded to briefly in Chapter Two. For the manager of an information services unit, being part of a project team in the community or organization of which the information services unit is a part is an excellent way to acquire advocates for yourself, as a managerial employee, and for the unit.

One of the best presentations of the value of team participation was provided in 1990 by Barb Pearson and Beth Soled, when they described their work as project team participants from the point of view of the specialized librarian in the research arm of a major corporation (Pearson and Soled, p. 18). All organizations, of course, whether private or public, put together project teams and special committees from time to time, usually for some specific purpose and for a set duration. The team, a 'group of individuals, each having a specific area of expertise, working jointly to accomplish a common goal', exists to provide the parent organization with some product or recommendation that will affect the operational goals and, as such, requires the highest level of expertise in each area. When members of a library or other information services agency are participants in project teams, they find that they are, in fact, the information specialists for the projects or, as Pearson and Soled say it, they 'provide the teams with information before they know they need it'.

There are, of course, other reasons for the information services manager and/or his staff to participate in such teams, and such rewards as being able to gain better understanding of the parent organization, the pleasures of participating in an important project, having a direct impact on organizational decisions, and having more control of information are all important reasons to accept an appointment to a project team, but the most important reason, of course, has to do with the visibility and the positive perceptions that such participation can bring to the specialized library or other information services unit. The unit becomes less vulnerable, and while the image of the unit is being improved, the other members of the team are becoming increasingly aware of the value of having an information specialist working with them.

For the information services manager who wants to participate in team projects (and all managers should), Pearson and Soled recommend seeking projects that are in the planning stage, so that the manager can participate in the entire project from the beginning. The point is to see the information manager's role as one of managing project information – a highly visible activity which will reflect well on the information services unit itself – so that the participation will create advocates and political supporters for the work of the information services unit.

In the final analysis, advocacy and political support are not really a choice for the progressive, innovative information services manager. As a manager, this person may be very self-motivated, may be willing to take any number of risks in order to provide the highest levels of service quality for the customers who come to take advantage of the products and services the unit has to offer, but in the long run, her job is made far easier by having others – interested non-professionals who understand the value of information – at her side, sharing her goals for the unit, and working with her to see that those goals are accorded the proper attention that they deserve. Without question, advocacy and political support activities are now part of the management picture for information services professionals. With appropriate care and development, advocates and political supporters can ease the way for the realization of the manager's goals for the information unit, in which case, all information stakeholders, the manager, her staff, the organization, and, especially, the users, succeed.

References

Bauer, Charles K. 'Managing management.' *Special Libraries*. 71 (4), April, 1980.

Berner, Andrew. 'Thinking about . . . Surviving the 90s.' *The One-Person Library: A Newsletter for Librarians and Management*. 6 (7), November, 1989.

Berner, Andrew, and St. Clair, Guy, eds. *The Best of OPL: Five Years of The One-Person Library*. Washington, DC: Special Libraries Association, 1990.

Berner, Andrew, and St. Clair, Guy. 'Reorganizational priorities for the private library: achieving excellence through change.' *Special Libraries*. 77 (4), Winter, 1987.

Bolef, Doris. 'The special library.' In: *The How-to-do-it Manual for Small Libraries*, edited by Bill Katz. New York: Neal-Schuman, 1988.

'EBIC'94: The European Business Information Conference, Paris, France, March 22–25, 1994.' *InfoManage: The International Management Newsletter for the Information Services Executive*. 1 (5) Supplement, April, 1994.

Esrey, William T. *Improving Productivity*. Address to the White House Conference on Library and Information Services. Washington, DC, July 10, 1991.

'Helping management get online.' *InfoManage: The International Management Newsletter for the Information Services Executive*. 1 (1), December, 1993.

Katayama, Jane H. 'The library committee: how important is it?' *Special Libraries*. 24 (1), 1983.

Labovitz, Judy. 'Managing a special library.' *Journal of Library Administration*. 6 (3), Fall, 1985.

Pearson, Barb, and Soled, Beth. 'How to be an integral part of a project team.' *PER Bulletin*. (Petroleum and Energy Resources Division, Special Libraries Association). 13 (2), 1990.

Shaughnessy, Thomas W. 'Making the boss more effective.' *Journal of Library Administration*. 8 (2), Summer, 1987.

White, Herbert S. *Managing the Special Library*. White Plains, NY: Knowledge Industry Publications, 1984.

Willard, Ann M. and Morrison, Patricia. 'The dynamic role of the information specialist.' *Special Libraries*. 79 (4), Fall, 1988.

Willner, Richard A. 'Education for library and information management careers in business and financial services.' *Library Trends*. 42 (2), Fall, 1993.

Power and influence in information services

Since the inception of the concepts described and discussed in this book, there have been any number of queries and comments about the title. 'Why?' it has been asked, sometimes facetiously. 'Why should there be a book on *power* and *influence* for librarians and information services personnel?'

In our society, the assumption seems to be that information providers are already characterized as people without power and influence, employees who exist to do the bidding of others, and any efforts to encourage them into positions of power and influence are somehow thought to be inappropriate.

Not so. Not in organizations and communities which have recognized, correctly, the value of information for the success of the organizational mission and the value of the people who can provide that information. It is this management recognition and its connection to participation in the creation of organizational values which drives information workers to seek power and influence. With power and influence (the same power and influence, incidentally, which enables other departments of organizations and other segments of society to attain their successes), librarians, records managers, archivists, information brokers, MIS staff, vendors, and all others involved in the organization, storage, and transfer of information are empowered to provide the best information services that can be provided and, at the same time, take their rightful role in organizational efforts that bring success to the organization or community as a whole.

So part of the goal here is to impress on the information services professional the value of *reputation* in the achievement of professional success. How one is perceived within the bounds of one's organization or community, the very entity that supports the library or other information services operation, is the essence of one's success. Much of that reputation comes, of course, with the level of information services and products provided for users, but just as important, much of it results from interactions with other decision makers and power brokers within the organization or community. To discount the place of reputation in the integration of information services into the organization as a whole, in this day and age and in our client-driven society, is short-sighted to the extreme and disarmingly naive.

Reputation and the perception of one's success lead to authority and freedom in the management of one's affairs and the affairs of the information services department for which one is responsible. Authority and influence are *enabling* forces in our society, and in the workplace. As concepts, authority and influence have been alluded to throughout this book, but it was an English information services expert who put forward perhaps the most compelling representation of the role that authority and influence play in our work.

Colin Offor describes authority and influence as the two 'key' elements of power within organizations. 'Politics in organizations,' he has written, 'is about the achievement and exercise of power. Whether that power is used to advance worthy or unworthy causes, the reality is that all organizations are riddled with politics, because all individuals at all levels seek to influence events to their advantage, and to enhance their position or prospects.' (Offor, pp. 139–140).

For the information services professional, the object is to achieve and exercise that power for the benefit of the information services operation for which he or she is responsible. It is not a question of personal pride (although some personal pride must come into the process), and it certainly is not a question of advancement within the organization or the community, for few information services professionals move out of information services into senior management positions. For the information services professional, particularly the information executive who has management authority for the provision of information products and services, the object is to provide the *best* products and services that enrich the organization or the community and enable it to succeed in the achievement of *its* mission.

In other words, in order to be ultimately successful within the organization, the information services professional *must* have power and influence, and if he or she does not, the services and products delivered from the unit will never be thought of as anything more than the products of an 'overhead' or 'storage' facility. To enhance the products and services emanating from the information services unit, to enable it to be more than simply a delivery operation, the professionals who work there must seek power and influence. Offor offers a reasonable and wise elaboration on this point:

> . . . If you become respected and successful within the organization you may begin to be involved in the control of it. You have what some people call power. Your life is still partly regulated by the actions and decisions of others, but now a part of it is regulated according to your own choice and by your own decisions. What you really have is freedom. . . . (Offor, p. 140)

The object, then, is to analyze – unemotionally and without fear or threat – everything we do as information services practitioners. We must step back and look at all our activities, first through the customer's eyes (to ensure that our operation is doing what it exists to do, providing the services and products that the customers need), and second, from our own point of view, as managers, to make some attempt to come up with a set of guidelines, a checklist, as it were, for achieving power and influence in the work we do.

As a first step, leading hopefully to the forming of these important guidelines, we might consider what two leaders in the information services profession, in separate discussions, have alluded to as a possible disadvantage in thinking about information users, the people who come to the information services unit for its products and services, as 'customers'. Although we want very much for our services and products, even the management of our information services operation, to be 'customer-focused' and 'customer-driven', we and our staff are, much of the time, put in a somewhat awkward position if we think of the users as 'customers' in the same sense that the business community thinks of the recipients of its products and services as 'customers'. On the other hand, attaching to these users the designation of 'reader', 'patron', and the like, as has been the case for the last hundred years or so in libraries and other information services agencies, is to put our own professionalism and our own expertise in jeopardy, for the connections with education and social work have effectively diminished the role of the information provider in this context to that of a subservient delivery agent, not expected to understand the subtle distinctions and 'hard-nosed' business practices of the 'real' world.

A useful and workable solution to this dilemma has come forth from both Anne P. Mintz and Angela Abell. Mintz, in a paper delivered to special librarians in November 1993, commented that the term 'customers' seems to put an artificial barrier between the information provider and the information user. She suggested instead that information services practitioners think of their users as 'colleagues', people within the organization – on an equal plane with the information provider – who just happen to have information needs. The information services operation, existing to provide information, meets those needs. Similarly, Abell, in a private conversation in London, expressed similar reservations and suggested the same designation. Obviously there is interest, within the information services community, for more of an organizational connection between the librarians, archivists, and other information services professionals and their 'colleagues' within the organization who, while working in different areas and seeking different successes, nevertheless are part of the same organizational effort. The suggestion is a useful one, for its enactment eliminates that first obstacle to achieving power and influence, the perception that the information services unit is separate and apart from the rest of the organization or community. So as a first guideline, we seek to think of our users as colleagues instead of as customers.

Other guidelines can be equally useful, and Colin Offor suggests seven (or eight, depending on whether one includes his final pointer about indispensability which, as we have seen, Ann Talcott – in Chapters Eight and Nine – would include). Offor asks, 'what can you do to increase your formal authority, have greater freedom of action, influence events in your own favor, and enhance your perceived significance?' His 'key rules' follow:

- Understand the culture.

- Read the runes.

- Know your limits of authority.

- Participate to the full.

- Cultivate the right people.

- Be versatile.

- Cultivate your charisma.

Offor notes that he was 'tempted' to add an eighth: to 'make yourself indispensable', which without question, is required for achieving power and influence in the organization served by the information services unit (Offor, pp. 143-144).

Continuing the quest for appropriate guidelines for acquiring power and influence within the organization, a look at an important paper by Nancy Prothro Norton provides much useful direction. Conceptualizing 'empowerment' in terms of Muriel B. Regan's very specific concept as 'understanding our potential to more influential in this information-driven society', Norton then defines the concept as 'an enabling process – a process of enabling oneself and others by enhancing personal efficacy' (Regan, p. 18, and Norton, pp. 119-124).

Norton then describes power in terms of three distinct types of power, 'each derived from a different source', and all of which 'have implications for the empowerment of information professionals'. They are *position* power, *knowledge* power, and *personal* power. The information services professional seeking to acquire power and influence within the organization must be able to recognize each of them.

Position power, for example, is 'legitimate power derived from one's official position in the organization'. As such, it confers a certain authority and, for librarians and other information services professionals, according to Norton, provides two advantageous roles in the application of position power obtained from their specific and unique skills. Information services professionals are 'gatekeepers of information flow', and, as such, 'can fashion usable management information from vast amounts of data'.

Norton has specific suggestions for the librarian/information services professional who would raise his or her 'power profile', and these can begin our list of guidelines for achieving power and influence within the organization:

1. Take on high visibility/high risk projects.

2. Develop information products or services targeted to top management.

3. Engage in creative problem solving in meeting user needs, and when this is done, it must be made known to the clients.

4. Set organizational information policy.

5. Control the budget and use it as a tool to promote the value of information services to the larger organization.

6. Become a strategic planner of the organization's infrastructure and share that vision with the larger organization.

7. Recognize the power of visibility.

8. Recognize the connections between what we do as information services professionals and a vision of what Peter Block in *The Empowered Manager* (p. 99) calls a 'vision of greatness'.

According to Norton, 'it is important the vision be grounded in the belief the profession has something to offer the larger organization that will, in Block's words, "truly make a difference". Block's prescriptive requirements for that vision seem to be created especially for the information profession: "pursue mastery, meaning, contribution, integrity, service."'

Norton defines knowledge power as 'a product of the person's unique expertise' and with this power, too, Norton has suggestions which can be guidelines for information services workers:

1. Develop and market services with more value-added components.

2. Establish themselves as information technology experts in the larger organization (introduce 'gee-whiz' technology whenever you can).

3. Charge for services – free services are undervalued.

4. Commit to lifelong learning.

Norton's third identified 'power type' is personal power, and she is quick to point out that there is a distinction between personal power and position power and knowledge power. The latter two (position power and knowledge power) are, as Norton has described them, a matter of *function*; personal power is a matter of *style*. So to be able to use personal power within the workplace, librarians and other information workers must become aware of their own personal styles, and, most important, must get rid of negative, 'librarian'-type traits.

Connected to Norton's suggestions might be yet another guideline for the assertive information services manager, to 'stretch' oneself, to continue to be excited by what you do and to think of one's role in the organization as that of an innovator and risk-taker. There is a critical piece to all of this concentration on power and influence, and it relates very specifically to how the information services manager and his or her staff feel about the work they do and the parent organization or community for which they work. In these days of flattened managerial structures, when the traditional divisiveness between labor and management is being consciously elimi-nated in the workplace, the information services manager and the people he or she supervises are now required to be enthusiastic and supportive of the organizations that employ them and to which they contribute their energies and effort for the organizational good. When these attributes – the 'stretching' of oneself and the recognition of the value of allegiance to the organization – are combined with those that Norton has identified for success in achieving power and influence within the organization, one begins to be recognized as a 'power player' and to acquire the authority and the freedom that Offor has written about.

Equally of value is one's relationship with one's immediate supervisor and with senior management as a whole. While nowadays we are all quick to proclaim that the user of the information service is the primary focus of our work (whether we call that person a 'customer' or a 'colleague'), the fact of the matter is that the *truly* important person in our work is the person to whom we report. As discussed earlier, that person is the person with whom we must achieve agreement in all that we do and, at the same time, we must recognize, realistically speaking, that the success of our work depends on our ability to keep that person happy. The manager of an information services operation *must* have a mutually supportive relation-ship with his or her immediate supervisor. Anything less is ultimately counterproductive, and every effort must be made, by the information services manager, to create that positive relationship if it does not exist and to enhance and build on it when it does.

In this context, yet another set of guidelines can be applied, and they come from the newsletter of the National Institute of Business Management (*On the Offensive*, p. 1). While these suggestions are not from the information services community, they can be applied with considerable success to information services work simply by making a few easy transfers of concepts and the easy application of these rules to an information environment instead of a business environment, and they should be considered. For example, one suggestion is that those seeking power within organizations should 'develop a specialty, a skill to complement whatever administrative post you hold'. This, of course, is exactly what information services work is, a specialty and a skill which no one else in the organization has and which can be exploited for the advantage of the information services unit.

A second guideline suggests that those seeking power should 'cultivate a

power look', and while librarians and other information services professionals often lament the lack of power, they are all too often unwilling
to observe how others around them – especially the decision makers – look
and deport themselves. Of course it is necessary to adjust one's 'look' to the
organizational culture that is in place, but it is nevertheless necessary, if one
aspires to power and influence within that organization, to understand the
value of 'looking the part', and acting accordingly.

A third suggestion adapted from the National Institute of Business Management encourages information services personnel, especially managers, to
'develop power contacts within your organization, people with information
that can help your accrual of power, or who are willing to support your ideas
in meetings or other public forums. Remember that information is power,
and the more you can lay your hands on – about suppliers, customers, good
temps, the "answer man" at corporate headquarters – the better off you are.'
Which comment, of course, like the development of a skill referred to above,
literally defines today's information services professional.

Another suggestion looks at the favors we do (as well as the services we
provide) for others: 'Know when to cash in your IOUs – and when not to.
Do enough discreet favors for people with access to power and you build
up a bank account of favor IOUs. These can then be bargained for better
assignments, trips with the brass, even raises and promotions.'

Nevertheless, this suggestion comes with its own warning: 'But be sure
the note is cashable before you try getting your "money", i.e., another favor.
If your IOU is based solely on expediting something you should have
done anyway, it can be hard to cash, and trying to do so could get you into
trouble.'

Another guideline has to do with strengthening the authority one already
has in place: 'Line up support from a credible outsider. Call in a consultant,
for example, to support your position in a disagreement. But try to pick
one more likely to back you than your opponent.'

Finally, in a point that cannot be argued too strongly or too seriously
within the information services context, it is suggested that those who are
successful in achieving power and influence within the organization 'always
stress the money angle'. Regardless of the type of organization in which the
information services unit operates, the financial returns engendered
through the presence of the information unit must be clearly stated and
understood by all decision makers, and it is the manager of the unit who has
the responsibility for conveying this information. The work connected with
the gathering of this information, the compilation of statistics, the follow-up
interviews after the information transaction has taken place, performance
evaluations of staff and services, and, especially, effectiveness measures
about the services and products provided by the information services unit
must not be shunted aside as 'nice-to-do' or optional tasks. Such activities,
and the reporting of the findings to the appropriate authorities within the
organization or community, are essential if the personnel working in

the information services unit are going to be perceived as having – and actually have – power and influence within the organization.

There are, then, any number of practical steps one can take in order to achieve for an information services operation a role of power and influence. While the guidelines listed here might work in some organizations and communities, others, just as sound, might be more effective in a different environment. The point is, there are ways for the managers and employees of an information services operation to achieve power and influence in the companies, organizations, and communities in which they work. While much of the effort can be directed to specific objectives connected to the efficient and effective delivery of information to information customers ('colleagues'), the true success of the endeavor will advance from the enthusiasm, vision, strategic planning, and strategic *management* of those information services professionals who bring to their work a commitment to provide the highest standards of service in the delivery of information products and services. For them, the acquisition of power and influence is a natural and normal part of the work they do.

References

Abell, Angela. Conversation with the author, April 29, 1994.

Block, Peter. *The Empowered Manager: Positive Political Skills at Work*. San Francisco, CA: Jossey-Bass, 1978.

Mintz, Anne P. 'Networking Within One's Organization.' Unpublished paper delivered at the Northeast Regional Conference, Special Libraries Association, November 4, 1993.

Norton, Nancy Prothro. 'Power to the information professional.' *Special Libraries*. 81 (2), Spring, 1990.

Offor, Colin. 'Your political base,' in *Management Skills for the Information Manager*, edited by Ann Lawes. Aldershot, England: Ashgate Publishing Limited, 1993.

'On the offensive: how to develop power-grabbing techniques that really work.' *Executive Strategies/Business-Personal*. New York: National Institute of Business Management, 1990.

Regan, Muriel B. 'Inaugural address.' *Annual Report, 1989–1990*. Washington, DC: Special Libraries Association, 1990.

Selected bibliography

Albrecht, Karl. *At America's Service: How Corporations can Revolutionize the Way they Treat their Customers*. Homewood, IL: Dow Jones-Irwin, 1988.

Albrecht, Karl, and Bradford, Lawrence J. *The Service Advantage: How to Identify and Fulfill Customer Needs*. Homewood, IL: Dow Jones-Irwin, 1990.

Asantewa, Doris. *Strategic Planning Basics for Special Libraries*. Washington, DC: Special Libraries Association, 1992.

Ashworth, Wilfred. *Special Librarianship*. London: Clive Bingley, 1979.

Atkinson, Philip E. *Creating Culture Change: The Key to Successful Total Quality Management*. Bedford, UK: IFS Ltd., 1990.

Barnard, Chester I. *Organization and Management*. Cambridge, MA: Harvard University Press, 1948.

Barrier, Michael. 'Small firms put quality first.' *Nation's Business*. 80 (5), May, 1992.

Bauer, Charles K. 'Managing management.' *Special Libraries*. 71 (4), April, 1980.

Bennis, Warren. *On Becoming a Leader*. Reading, MA: Addison-Wesley, 1989.

Bennis, Warren, and Nanus, Burt. *Leaders: The Strategies for Taking Charge*. New York: Harper and Row, 1985.

Berner, Andrew. 'Thinking about . . . surviving the 90s.' *The One-Person Library: A Newsletter for Librarians and Management*. 6 (7), November, 1989.

Berner, Andrew, and St. Clair, Guy. 'Reorganizational priorities for the private library: achieving excellence through change.' *Special Libraries*. 77 (4), Winter, 1987.

Berner, Andrew, and St. Clair, Guy, eds. *The Best of OPL: Five Years of The One-Person Library*. Washington, DC: Special Libraries Association, 1990.

Block, Peter. *The Empowered Manager: Positive Political Skills at Work*. San Francisco, CA: Jossey-Bass, 1978.

Bolef, Doris. 'The special library,' in *The How-to-do-it Manual for Small Libraries*, edited by Bill Katz. New York: Neal-Schuman, 1988.

Bradford, David, and Cohen, Allan. *Managing for Excellence*. New York: John Wiley and Sons, 1984.

Burkett, J. 'Library and information services,' in *Handbook of Special Librarianship and Information Work*, edited by L.J. Anthony. London: Aslib, 1982.

Butler, Meredith, and Davis, Hiram. 'Strategic planning as a catalyst for change in the 1990s.' *College & Research Libraries*. 53, September, 1992, (pp. 393–403).

Cargill, Jennifer. 'Developing library leaders: the role of mentorship.' *Library Administration and Management*. Winter, 1989.

Curzon, Susan C. *Managing Change: A How-to-do-it Manual for Planning, Implementing and Evaluating Change in Libraries*. New York: Neal-Schuman, 1989.

Dalziel, Murray M., and Schoonover, Stephen C. *Changing Ways: A Practical Tool for Implementing Change Within Organizations*. New York: American Management Association, 1988.

Deal, Terrence, and Kennedy, Allan. *Corporate Cultures: The Rites and Rituals of Corporate Life*. Reading, MA: Addison-Wesley, 1982.

Drake, David. 'When your boss isn't a librarian.' *American Libraries*. February, 1990.

Drake, Miriam A. 'Value of the information professional: cost/benefit analysis.' *President's Task Force on the Value of the Information Professional, Final Report, Preliminary Study, June 10, 1987*. Washington, DC: Special Libraries Association, 1987.

Drucker, Peter F. *The New Realities*. New York: HarperCollins, 1989.

Drucker, Peter F. *Managing the Nonprofit Organization: Principles and Practices*. New York: HarperCollins, 1990.

Drucker, Peter F. *Post-Capitalist Society*. New York: HarperCollins, 1993.

'EBIC'94: The European Business Information Conference, Paris, France, March 22–25, 1994.' *InfoManage: The International Management Newsletter for the Information Services Executive*. 1 (5) Supplement, April, 1994.

Echelman, Shirley. 'Libraries are businesses too.' *Special Libraries*. 65, October/November, 1974.

Eddison, Elizabeth Bole. 'The entrepreneur as change agent: innovation through product and service genesis,' in *Agents of Change: Progress and Innovation in the Library/Information Profession*, edited by Jana Varlejs. Jefferson, NC: McFarland and Company, 1992.

Ertel, Monica. 'Getting a piece of the pie: R&D at the Apple Library.' *Library Journal*. September 15, 1990 (pp. 40–44).

Esrey, William T. '*Improving Productivity: Address to the White House Conference on Library and Information Services*.' Washington, DC: National Commission on Libraries and Information Services, July 10, 1991.

Ettinger, Andrew. 'From information to total quality learning: How the information profession needs to change to meet new challenges.' A presentation at the conference on 'The value of information to the intelligent organization,' University of Hertfordshire, Hatfield, UK, September 8, 1993. Described in *InfoManage: The International*

Management Newsletter for the Information Services Executive. 1 (1), December, 1993.

Ferguson, Elizabeth, and Mobley, Emily R. *Special Libraries at Work*. Hamden, CT: The Shoe String Press, 1984.

Ferriero, David S. and Wilding, Thomas L. 'Scanning the Environment in Strategic Planning.' *Masterminding Tomorrow's Information - Creative Strategies for the '90s: Professional Papers from the 82nd Annual Conference of the Special Libraries Association, San Antonio, TX, June 8-13, 1991*. Washington, DC: Special Libraries Association, 1991.

Fredenburg, Anne M. 'Quality assurance: establishing a program for special libraries.' *Special Libraries*. 79 (4), Fall, 1988.

Gardner, John W. *The Nature of Leadership*. Washington, DC: Independent Sector, 1986.

Garfield, John. *Peak Performers: The New Heroes of American Business*. New York: Morrow, 1986.

Griffiths, José-Marie, and King, Donald W. *A Manual on the Evaluation of Information Centers and Services*. New York: The American Institute of Aeronautics and Astronautics, 1991.

Hamilton, Feona. 'The information audit,' in *Management Skills for the Information Manager*, edited by Ann Lawes. London: Ashgate, 1993.

Harps, Leslie. 'Using Customer Service to Keep Subscribers.' A Presentation to the Newsletter Publishers Association, Washington, DC, January 21, 1992 (unpublished).

'Helping management get online.' *InfoManage: The International Management Newsletter for the Information Services Executive*. 1 (1), December, 1993.

Hobrock, Brice G. 'Creating your library's future through effective strategic planning.' *Journal of Library Administration*. 14 (2), 1991 (pp. 37ff.).

Horton, Forest Woody. *Extending the Librarian's Domain: A Survey of Emerging Occupation Opportunities for Librarians and Information Professionals*. Washington, DC: Special Libraries Association, 1994.

The Human Side of Quality: People, Pride, Performance. Milwaukee, WI: American Society for Quality Control, 1990.

Jones, Cathy. 'The information interview: it's the Staff - Catherine A. Jones talks about LC's Congressional Reference Division.' *InfoManage: The International Management Newsletter for the Information Services Executive*. 1 (2), January, 1994 (pp. 2-3).

Kanter, Rosabeth Moss. *The Change Masters: Innovation and Entrepreneurship in the American Corporation*. New York: Simon and Schuster, 1983.

Katayama, Jane H. 'The library committee: how important is it?' *Special Libraries*. 24 (1), 1983.

Kilmann, Ralph M. *Managing Beyond the Quick Fix*. San Francisco, CA: Jossey-Bass, 1989.

Kok, John. '"Now that I'm in charge, what do I do?" Six rules about running a special library for the new library manager. *Special Libraries*. 71 (4), December, 1980.

Labovitz, Judy. 'Managing a special library.' *Journal of Library Administration*. 6 (3), Fall, 1985.

LaRosa, Sharon. 'In pursuit of partnership.' *MLS: Marketing Library Services*. 7 (3), April/May, 1993.

Lawes, Ann. 'The information interview: what's expected of an information services executive? In the UK, Ann Lawes has some answers.' *InfoManage: The International Management Newsletter for the Information Services Executive*. Prototype issue, June, 1993.

Leonard, W. Patrick. 'This year is different: Facing outcome assessment.' *Journal of Academic Librarianship*. 18, September, 1992.

Levitt, Theodore. *Thinking about Management*. New York: Free Press, 1991.

Manning, Helen. 'The corporate librarian: great return on investment.' *President's Task Force on the Value of the Information Professional*. Washington, DC: Special Libraries Association, 1987.

Marshall, Joanne G. *The Impact of the Special Library on Corporate Decision-Making*. Washington, DC: Special Libraries Association, 1993.

Matarazzo, James M., Prusak, Laurence, and Gauthier, Michael R. *Valuing Corporate Libraries: A Survey of Senior Managers*. Washington, DC: Special Libraries Association, 1990.

Mintz, Anne P. 'Networking Within One's Organization.' Unpublished paper delivered at the Northeast Regional Conference, Special Libraries Association, November 4, 1993.

Morton, Phillip W. 'The information manager: a link in effective organizational decision making,' in *Managing the Electronic Library: Papers of the 1982 Conference of the Library Management Division of the Special Libraries Association*, edited by Michael Koenig. New York: Special Libraries Association, 1983.

Mount, Ellis. *Special Libraries and Information Centers: An Introductory Text*. Washington, DC: Special Libraries Association, 1991.

Newsome, James, and McInerney, Claire. 'Environmental scanning and the information manager.' *Special Libraries*. 81 (4), Fall, 1990.

Norton, Nancy Prothro. 'Power to the information professional.' *Special Libraries*. 81 (2), Spring, 1990.

Odiorne, George. *How Managers Make Things Happen*. Englewood Cliffs, NJ: Prentice Hall, 1982.

O'Donnell, William S. 'The vulnerable corporate special library/ information center: minimizing the risks.' *Special Libraries*. 67, April, 1976 (pp. 179–187).

Offor, Colin. 'Your political base,' in *Management Skills for the Information Manager*, edited by Ann Lawes. Aldershot, England: Ashgate, 1993.

'On the offensive: How to develop power-grabbing techniques that really work.' *Executive Strategies/Business-Personal*. New York: National Institute of Business Management, August 21, 1990.

Orna, Elizabeth. 'Should we educate our users?' *Aslib Proceedings*. 30 (4), 1978.

Orna, Elizabeth. *Practical Information Policies: How to Manage Information Flow in Organizations*. Aldershot, England: Ashgate, 1990.

Palmer, Richard Phillips, and Varnet, Harvey. *How to Manage Information: A Systems Approach*. Phoenix, AZ: Oryx Press, 1990.

Palmour, Vernon El, et al. *A Planning Process for Public Libraries*. Chicago, IL: American Library Association, 1980.

Pascarella, Perry. *The New Achievers*. New York: The Free Press, 1984.

Paul, Meg. 'Improving service provision.' *The Australian Library Journal*. 22 (10), November, 1991 (p. 65).

Paul, Meg. 'Why special libraries close: A consultant's view.' *Australian Special Library News*. 26 (4), December, 1993.

Pearson, Barb, and Soled, Beth. 'How to be an integral part of a project team.' *PER Bulletin* (Petroleum and Energy Resources Division, Special Libraries Association). 13 (2), 1990.

Penniman, W. David. 'Shaping the future: The Council on Library Resources helps to fund change.' *Library Journal*. 117 (17), 1992 (pp. 40–45).

Peters, Tom. *Thriving on Chaos*. New York: Knopf, 1987.

Peters, Tom. *Liberation Management: Necessary Disorganization for the Nanosecond Nineties*. New York: Knopf, 1992.

Peters, Tom, and Waterman, Robert. *In Search of Excellence: Lessons from America's Best-Run Companies*. New York: Harper and Row, 1982.

Pfeffer, Jeffrey. *Managing With Power: Politics and Influence in Organizations*. Boston, MA: Harvard Business School Press, 1994.

Regan, Muriel B. 'Inaugural address.' *Annual Report, 1989–1990*. Washington, DC: Special Libraries Association, 1990.

Riggs, Donald E. 'Making creative, innovative, and entrepreneurial things happen in a special library.' *Journal of Library Administration*. 10 (2/3), 1989.

Rollwagen, John. 'Washington: News from the front.' *Inc. Magazine*. 16 (1), January, 1994.

Rosser, M. James, and Penrod, James I. 'Strategic planning and management: A methodology for responsible change.' *Journal of Library Administration*. 13 (3/4), 1990.

Sager, Donald J. *Managing the Public Library*. Boston, MA: G.K. Hall, 1989.

St. Clair, Guy. 'Your library advocates: Do you benefit from them?' *The One-Person Library: A Newsletter for Librarians and Management*. 3 (10/11), February–March, 1987.

St. Clair, Guy. 'Commitment, courage and a lot of heart.' *Bibliotheca Medica Canadiana*. 9 (3), 1988.

St. Clair, Guy. *Customer Service in the Information Environment*. London: Bowker-Saur, 1993.

Schein, Edgar. *Organizational Culture and Leadership: A Dynamic View*. San Francisco, CA and London: Jossey-Bass, 1985.

Shaughnessy, Thomas W. 'Making the boss more effective.' *Journal of Library Administration*. 8 (2), Summer, 1987.

Shaughnessy, Thomas W. 'Organizational culture in libraries.' *Journal of Library Administration*. 9 (3), 1988.

Shea, Gordon F. *Company Loyalty: Earning It, Keeping It*. New York: American Management Association, 1987.

Silverzweig, Stan, and Allen, Robert. 'Changing the corporate culture.' *Sloan Management Review*. Spring, 1976.

Sirkin, Arlene Farber. 'Marketing planning for maximum effectiveness.' *Special Libraries*. 82 (1), Winter, 1991.

Strable, Edward G. 'Special libraries: How are they different?' *Illinois Libraries*. 62, March, 1980.

Swanigan, Meryl. 'Managing a special library.' *Journal of Library Administration*. 6 (3), Fall, 1985.

Szilagyi, Andrew D., Jr. *Management and Performance*. Glenview, IL: Scott, Foresman and Company, 1988.

Talcott, Ann. 'Managing electronic libraries,' in *Managing the Electronic Library: Papers of the 1982 Conference of the Library Management Division of the Special Libraries Association*, edited by Michael Koenig. New York: Special Libraries Association, 1983.

Talcott, Ann. 'Indispensable or Expendable? Making Yourself Valuable to Your Organization.' Unpublished paper presented at the Special Libraries Association Northeast Regional Conference, November 3, 1993.

'A tale of two corporate libraries.' *InfoManage: The International Management Newsletter for the Information Services Executive*. 1 (3), February, 1994.

Turock, Betty J. 'Valuing information services,' in *The Bottom Line Reader: A Financial Handbook for Librarians*. New York: Neal-Schuman, 1990.

Varlejs, Jana, ed. *Agents of Change: Progress and Innovation in the Library/Information Profession*. [Proceedings of the Twenty-ninth Annual Symposium of the Graduate Alumni and Faculty of the Rutgers School of Communication, Information and Library Studies, 12 April 1992]. Jefferson, NC: McFarland and Company, 1992.

Veaner, Allen B. 'Introduction.' *President's Task Force on the Value of the Information Professional, Final Report, Preliminary Study*. Washington, DC: Special Libraries Association, 1987.

Vogelsang, Marlene. 'The reflection of corporate culture in the library or information center.' *Library Management Quarterly*. 12 (2), Spring, 1989.

Vincent, Ida. 'Strategic planning and libraries: Does the model fit?' *Journal of Library Administration*. 9 (3), 1988 (p. 35ff.).

Waldron, Helen J. 'The business of running a special library.' *Special Libraries*. 62, February, 1971.

Watson, Tom G. 'The librarian as change agent.' *Advances in Library Administration and Organization*. 2, 1983.

Welch, Bettiann. 'Marketing: Winning customers with a "workable" plan.' *Success Magazine*. June, 1990.

White, Herbert S. *Managing the Special Library: Strategies for Success Within the Larger Organization*. White Plains, NY: Knowledge Industry Publications, 1984.

White, Herbert S. 'Management: A strategy for change.' *Canadian Library Journal*. October, 1978. Reprinted in White, Herbert S. *Librarians and the Awakening From Innocence: A Collection of Papers*. Boston, MA: G.K. Hall and Company, 1989.

White, Lawrence. 'The sensible economist's guide to the economics of information,' in *The Economics of Information: Proceedings of the Twentieth Annual Symposium Sponsored by the Alumni and Faculty of the Rutgers Graduate School of Library and Information Studies, April 3, 1981*. Jefferson, NC: McFarland & Company, 1982.

Willard, Ann M. and Morrison, Patricia. 'The dynamic role of the information specialist: Two perspectives.' *Special Libraries*. 79 (4), Fall, 1988 (pp. 271-276).

Willner, Richard A. 'Education for library and information management careers in business and financial services.' *Library Trends*. 42 (2), Fall, 1993.

Woodsworth, Anne, and Williams, James F. II. *Managing the Economics of Owning, Leasing and Contracting Out Information Services*. Aldershot, England, and Brookfield, VT: Ashgate, 1993.

Wright, Craig. 'Corporate records management and the librarian.' *Special Libraries*. 82 (4), Fall, 1991.

Zaleznik, Abraham. 'Managers and leaders: Are they different?' *Harvard Business Review*. May-June, 1977.

Zemke, Ron, and Schaaf, Dick. *The Service Edge*. New York: Penguin Books USA, 1989.

Index